GETTING BY IN HEBREW

A quick beginners' course for tourists and businesspeople

by
Prof. Moshe Pelli
Department of Hebrew Literature
Yeshiva University

BARRON'S
Woodbury, New York/London/Toronto/Sydney

All inquiries should be addressed to:
Barron's Educational Series, Inc.
113 Crossways Park Drive
Woodbury, New York 11797

Library of Congress Catalog Card No. 83-22435

International Standard Book No. 0-8120-2662-4

Library of Congress Cataloging in Publication Data

Pelli, Moshe.
Getting by in Hebrew.

1. Hebrew language—Conversation and phrase books—English. I. Title.
PJ4573.P39 1984 492.4'83421 83-22435
ISBN 0-8120-2662-4

PRINTED IN THE UNITED STATES OF AMERICA

Series Editors: Ruth Pecan, Barbara Gilson, Carole Berglie
Consultants: Jeffrey Weill, H. Z. Szubin, Yael Feldman
Illustrator: Juan Suarez

4567 550 987654321

Contents

SYRIA
Jordan River
Haifa
MEDITERRANEAN
SEA
Tel Aviv
Jerusalem
Gaza Strip
DEAD SEA
BEERSHEVA
ISRAEL
JORDAN
Negev
EGYPT
GULF OF ELAT (AQABA)

The course . . . and how to use it

Getting by in Hebrew is a five-unit self-study crash course for anyone planning to visit Israel, or for anyone interested in learning to speak basic Hebrew. The course has been designed to give you, in a short period, a basic 'survival kit' for some of the situations typical of a visit to Israel.

'Getting by' means

- □ managing to keep your head above water
- □ having a try at making yourself understood
- □ listening for clues so that you can get the gist of what people say to you
- □ knowing how to take shortcuts—and get what you want
- □ knowing how to look up what you don't understand
- □ getting more fun out of your trip abroad

Each Unit

- □ concentrates on the language you'll need to use and understand to cope with a particular situation—getting something to eat and drink, booking a room in a hotel, going shopping, asking the way. . .
- □ includes real-life conversations, specially recorded by native Israelis, to let you hear Hebrew right from the start
- □ teaches you to speak the minimum you need to 'get by'—the simple sentences that are useful in a variety of situations
- □ gives you an opportunity to repeat new words and expressions aloud in the pauses left on the cassettes
- □ helps you pick out the key information in what people say without worrying about the exact meaning of every word

The cassettes

- allow you to repeat new words and phrases
- enable you to proceed at your own pace
- let you imitate native speakers
- review each unit for you to check your own progress

The study book includes

- the text of the conversations recorded on the cassettes both in transliteration (the sound of Hebrew presented in English script) and in the original Hebrew alphabet
- a summary of what you'll need to say, and to listen for
- brief language explanations
- tips about everyday life in Israel

At the end of the book there is a section containing a guide to pronunciation in Hebrew and to the system of transliteration used in this book; cross references to where you'll find numbers, days of the week, emergency phone numbers, and so on, in the Worth Knowing sections; additional useful information on the metric system, measurements, weights, temperatures, the Hebrew alphabet, and word lists.

To make the most of the course

As you listen to the recorded conversations on the cassette, try to get used to the sound of Hebrew without looking at the book. Then read through the unit in the book, and proceed section by section. Get acquainted with the system of transliteration at the end of the book, to make it easy for you to read Hebrew in English script and to pronounce words and phrases properly.

- While you listen to the cassettes, take every opportunity to repeat aloud the words and expressions you are asked to say, and concentrate on listening for clues. Saying the words aloud will not only help you get the sounds right, but will make it easier for you to remember the words and phrases. It will also give you some needed confidence in speaking.

- On the cassettes the pauses for your replies are timed to allow for a little thought but a fairly prompt answer. If the pauses seem too short at first, lengthen them by stopping the tape recorder.

After listening to each unit, work through the chapter in the study book. Read the conversations aloud, with someone else if possible. If he or she is also your partner on the trip, both of you can benefit from these language practices. Go through the Language Summary and Explanations sections in each unit. Check new words and phrases in the Key Words and Phrases sections in each unit, or in the word lists at the end of the book. Review the material thoroughly, and read through the notes.

Study habits

Everyone has a personal way of learning, and as you work through the course, you'll find the best way suited to you. Much will depend on whether you're using the cassettes. Learning a language requires frequent practice. A good rule of thumb is to do a little, often. When you're on your own, driving to work or doing some chore around the house, listen again to the cassette and talk Hebrew to yourself. If something seems difficult the first time around, it will get easier as you review the units and as you progress through the chapters.

When you go abroad take this study book with you, plus a good up-to-date pocket dictionary and a notebook, so that you may jot down words and phrases you discover on your own.

If you can *Get by in Hebrew*, you'll enjoy your visit all the more! *Nesi'ah ne'imah*!

1 Getting to know people

Conversations

The conversations are included in the introduction to Unit One. The purpose of presenting them to you at this early stage is to acquaint you with the sound of Hebrew as it is spoken by native Israelis. Listen to the dialogues. You are not expected to understand the conversations yet but to get used to the 'music' of the language, its intonation, its tone, and its rhythm. So, sit back, relax, and listen to how the following situations sound in Hebrew.

Meeting people

Mr. Rosen Shalóm.
שלום.

Mr. Cohen Shalóm.
שלום.

Mr. Rosen Mah shlomćha, mar Ćohen?
מה שלומְךָ, מר כהן?

Mr. Cohen Tov, tođah. (*To Mrs. Brown*)
טוב, תודה.

Uḿah shloḿech, gevéret Brown?
ומה שלומֵךְ, גברת בץ?

Mrs. Brown Tov me'ód, tođah.
טוב מאוד, תודה.

Ordering a drink

Waiter Mah tishťeh? Aťah rotzeh
מה תשתה? אתה רוצה

tei o kafe?
תה או קפה?

Customer Kafe, bevakaśhah.
קפה, בבקשה.

Asking where the telephone is

Stranger Éifo haťelefon?
איפה הטלפון?

Friend Hat́elefon baĺobi.

הטלפון בַּלוֹבִּי.

Changing money

Customer Efśhar lehaḥaĺif ḱesef?

אפשר להחליף כסף?

Waiter Ken. Yesh lećha t́ravelers cheks?

כן. יש לך טרוולרס צ׳קס?

Booking a hotel room

Tourist Yesh laćhem ḥ́eder pańuy?

יש לכם חדר פנוי?

Clerk Ken. Yesh ĺanu ḥ́eder pańuy. At́ah rot́zeh ḥeder leyaḥ́id o leźug?

כן. יש לנו חדר פנוי. אתה
רוצה חדר ליחיד או לזוג?

Tourist Ḥ́eder leźug, bevakaśhah.

חדר לזוג, בבקשה.

Finding your way

Tourist Eich ańi maǵi'a lakonśulyah ha'ameriḱa'it?

איך אני מגיע לקונסוליה
האמריקאית?

Stranger Lech yaśhar ad sof hareḥ́ov; pneh yaḿinah, ve'aḥ́ar kach yaśhar sḿolah.

לֵך ישר עד סוף הרחוב; פְּנֵה
ימינה, ואחר כך ישר שמאלה.

Listen to familiar words

Border police Passṕort, bevakaśhah.

פספורט, בבקשה.

Stranger Éifo hat́elefon?

איפה הטלפון?

Friend Hat́elefon baĺobi.

הטלפון בלובי.

Listen to the tone of voice

Tourist	Yesh laćhem ḥeder pańuy? יש לכם חדר פנוי?
Clerk I	Lo. Ein ĺanu ḥeder pańuy. לא. אין לנו חדר פנוי.
Clerk II	Ken. Yesh ĺanu ḥeder pańuy. כן. יש לנו חדר פנוי.
Teller	Yesh lećha ťravelers cheks? יש לך טרוולרס צ׳קס?
Tourist	Ken. Yesh li ťravelers cheks. כן. יש לי טרוולרס צ׳קס.

English words in Hebrew

lobi	לוֹבִּי	oto	אוטו
radyo	רדיו	limon	לימון
taksi	טקסי	sendvitch	סנדוויץ׳
bank	בנק	kafe	קפה
chek	צ׳ק	tei	תה
travelers	טרוולרס		
cheks	צ׳קס		

English words modified in Hebrew

televizyah	טלוויזיה	diyetah	דיאטה
telegramah	טלגרמה	birah	בירה

Conversations

These are the texts of the conversations included in this unit. After you listen to the cassettes, read the conversations aloud as often as you can. Acquaint yourself with the pronunciation guide at the end of the book so that you can follow the transliteration as easily as possible. Before attempting to converse in Hebrew, you may prefer to go through the Language Summary and Explanations sections found in each unit. Words underlined in the Conversations are the absolute minimum you need to say to 'get by.'

On the right-hand side you'll find the text printed in the Hebrew alphabet. You are not expected to master it. However, those who have had some background in Hebrew and are able to read it, are encouraged to try the right-hand column occasionally. Others may wish to get to know the Hebrew alphabet (see the reference section at the end of the book) so that they can read and understand simple road signs and street names.

Key words and phrases

Shalom	Hello, hi, goodbye
Mar, adon	Mr.
Geveret	Mrs.
Mah shlomcha	How are you? (to a male)
Mah shlomech	How are you? (to a female)
Tov	Good
Tov me'od	Very good
Metzuyan	Excellent
Todah	Thank (you)
Beseder	O.K., fine
Hakol beseder	Everything is O.K.
Boker tov	Good morning
Erev tov	Good evening
Laylah tov	Good night
Shabat shalom	Good Sabbath; have a peaceful Sabbath
Ḥag same'aḥ	Have a happy holiday

Saying hello

Tourist	Shalóm, mar Cóhen.	שלום, מר כהן.
	or	
Tourist	Shalóm, adón Cóhen.	שלום, אדון כהן.
Tourist	Shalóm, gevéret Cóhen.	שלום, גברת כהן.

. . . and goodbye

Tourist	Shalóm.	שלום.

Being asked how you are

Tourist	Mah shlomcha, mar Cohen?	מה שלומְךָ, מר כהן?
	or	
Tourist	Mah shlomcha, adón Cohen?	מה שלומךָ, אדון כהן?
Tourist	Mah shlomech, gevéret Cohen?	מה שלומךְ, גברת כהן?

. . . and replying

Tourist	Tov, todáh.	טוב, תודה.
	better:	
Tourist	Tov me'ód, todáh.	טוב מאוד, תודה.
	even better:	
Tourist	Metzuýan.	מצויין.
	O.K.	
Tourist	Beseder.	בסדר.
	Fine:	
Tourist	Hakol beséder.	הכול בסדר.

Saying good morning

Tourist Bóker tov.

בוקר טוב.

. . . good evening

Tourist Érev tov.

ערב טוב.

. . . and good night

Tourist Láylah tov.

לילה טוב.

Greetings on the Sabbath

Tourist Shabát shalóm.

שבת שלום.

. . . and on the holidays

Tourist Ḥag saméʼaḥ.

חג שמח.

. . . at the dinner table

Man Érev tov. Mah shlomḗch?

ערב טוב. מה שלומךְ?

Woman Tov, tódah.

טוב, תודה.

. . . and at the breakfast table

Man Bóker tov, mar Brown.

בוקר טוב, מר בראון.

Man Mah shloméch, gévèret Brown?

מה שלומךְ, גברת בראון?

Woman Tov me'ód.

טוב מאוד.

Key words and phrases

Mah tishteh? What would you like to drink?
Atah rotzeh (Do) you want (to a male)

Tei o kafe	Tea or coffee
Kafe shaḥor	Black coffee
Kafe turki	Turkish coffee
Nes kafe	Instant coffee
Espresso	Espresso
Tei im limon	Tea with lemon
O	Or
Im ḥalav	With milk
Ugah	Cake
Ken	Yes
Ugat gevinah	Cheese cake
Ugat tapuḥim	Apple cake
Ugat duvdevanim	Cherry cake
Rotzah	Want (feminine)

Ordering a drink

Waiter Bóker tov.

בוקר טוב.

Customer Bóker tov.

בוקר טוב.

Waiter Mah tishtéh? Atáh rotzéh tei o kafé?

מה תשתה? אתה רוצה תה או קפה?

Getting coffee

Customer Kafé, bevakaśhah.

קפה, בבקשה.

Waiter Kafé shaḥor? Kafé Turki? Nes kafe? O espŕesso?

קפה שחור? קפה טורקי? נס קפה?
או אספרסו?

Customer Kafé turḱi, bevakaśhah.

קפה טורקי, בבקשה.

. . . and tea

Customer Tei, bevakaśhah.

תה, בבקשה.

Waiter Tei im limón o im ḥaláv?

תה עם לימון או עם חלב?

Customer Tei im limón, bevakaśhah.

תה עם לימון, בבקשה.

. . . and cake

Waiter	Aťah roťzeh uǵah?
	אתה רוצה עוגה?
Customer	Ken.
	כן.
Waiter	Uǵat geviňah, uǵat tapuḥim, o uǵat duvdevaňim?
	עוגת גבינה, עוגת תפוחים, או עוגת דובדבנים?
Customer	Uǵat geviňah, bevakaśhah.
	עוגת גבינה, בבקשה.
Waiter	Mah roťzah hageveret?
	מה רוצָה הגברת?
Customer	Uǵat tapuḥim, bevakaśhah.
	עוגת תפוחים, בבקשה.
	or
	Hageveret roťzah uǵat tapuḥim.
	הגברת רוצָה עוגת תפוחים.

Key words and phrases

Meltzar	Waiter
Meltzarit	Waitress
Ḥeshbon	Bill, check
Efshar leshalem?	Can I pay?
Efshar lehaḥalif . . . ?	Can I change . . . ?
Kesef	Money
Yesh lecha . . . ?	(Do) you have . . . ? (to a male)
Yesh li	I have

Paying the bill

Customer	Meltzar! Ḥeshbon, bevakaśhah!
	מלצר! חשבון, בבקשה!
	addressing a waitress:
Customer	Meltzarit! Ḥeshbon, bevakaśhah!
	מלצרית! חשבון,בבקשה!
	. . . and another way:
Customer	Meltzar. Efśhar leshalem?
	מלצר. אפשר לשלם?

. . . and changing money

Customer	Efshar lehaḥalíf késef? אפשר להחליף כסף?
Waiter	Ken. Yesh lećha tŕavelers cheks? כן. יש לך טרוולרס צ׳קס?
Customer	Ken. Yesh li tŕavelers cheks. כן. יש לי טרוולרס צ׳קס.

Assignment for next time

Figure out how to order a sandwich and beer from the waiter.

Language summary

What you need to say

How to say 'hello' . . .

Shalom	*any time*
Boker tov	*in the morning*
Erev tov	*in the evening*

. . . and 'goodbye'

Shalom	*any time*

Asking how someone is

Mah shlom-cha?	*to a male*
Mah shlo-mech?	*to a female*

. . . and telling how you are

Tov	*when you feel well*
Tov me'od	*when you feel very well*
Hakol beseder	*when every-thing is O.K.*

How to accept something
Ken, todah

. . . or refuse politely
Lo, todah

Ordering something to drink
Kafe, bevakashah
Kafe shaḥor, bevakashah

Kafe turki, bevakashah
Nes kafe, bevakashah
Kafe espresso, bevakashah
Kafe im ḥalav, bevakashah

Tei, bevakashah
Tei im limon, bevakashah
Tei im ḥalav, bevakashah

Calling the waiter or waitress . . .
Meltzar!
Meltzarit!

. . . and asking for the bill
Ḥeshbon, bevakashah!
Efshar leshalem?

Changing money
Efshar lehaḥalif kesef?
Ken. Yesh li travelers cheks.

What you need to listen for

Being asked what you want
Mah tishteh?
Atah rotzeh tei o kafe?
Tei im limon o im ḥalav?
Atah rotzeh ugah?
Mah rotzah hageveret?

Being asked what money you want to change
Yesh lecha travelers cheks?

Explanations

The definite article

The definite article 'the' is *ha* in Hebrew (pronounced, at certain times also as *he*). It precedes and is joined to both the noun and the modifying adjective. Thus the noun *telefon* becomes *hatelefon* and *geveret* becomes *hageveret*. There is no indefinite article in Hebrew. *A* telephone is *telefon*.

Gender

In Hebrew, gender is very important. **Nouns,** whether people or things, are either masculine or feminine. Most words ending with *ah* are feminine: *televizyah, telegramah, birah, ugah.* (Words ending in *it* and *et* also are feminine, as in *meltzarit* and *geveret.*) Words with other endings are usually masculine: *lobi, radyo, ḥeshbon, erev, boker*. There are, of course, exceptions to this rule. *Laylah*, for example, has a feminine ending but is masculine. When you learn a new word, try also to learn what gender it is.

Verbs also have masculine and feminine endings to show the speaker or the person addressed: *Atah rotzeh* ('Do you want') is masculine. *Hageveret rotzah* is the feminine form. The pronoun, 'you,' has four forms in Hebrew:

atah	masculine singular	*atem*	masculine plural
at	feminine singular	*aten*	feminine plural

Adjectives agree in gender with the nouns they describe: *boker tov*—'*good* morning,' or *shanah tovah*—'*good* New Year.'

Word order

Adjectives follow the nouns they describe: *boker tov, kafe shaḥor*. The same rule applies to adverbs: *tov me'od*—'*very* good,' and to **verbs:** *atah rotzeh*—'you *want*.'

Questions

Mah tishteh?	*What would you like to drink?*
Mah rotzah hageveret?	*What* does the lady want?
Efshar leshalem?	*Can* I (Is it possible to) pay?

Questions may be indicated by reverse order of noun and verb.

Negation

The negation of *yesh lanu*—'we have', is *ein lanu*—'we do not have.' The normal word to indicate the negative is *lo*—'no.'

Worth knowing

Greetings

Shalom means different things to different people. *Shalom* means 'peace' and is part of the name of Jerusalem (*Yerushalayim* or *Yerushalem*), which means 'a city of peace.' It is used as a greeting as well as to say goodbye. When you say *shalom* in greeting someone, you actually say 'may peace be with you.' When you ask someone *Mah shlomcha?*—'how are you?,' you actually inquire 'What is the state of your well-being?'

When you greet someone with *shabat shalom*, you wish him a 'Sabbath of peace' or a 'peaceful Sabbath.' There are other greetings on special occasions. At the end of the day you may hear the greeting, *leil menuḥah*—'have a restful night.' The last news broadcast in Kol Yisra'el (the Israeli radio), at one in the morning, ends with the words: *Leil menuḥah mirushalayim*—'wishing you a restful night from Jerusalem.'

At the end of the Jewish Sabbath, you may hear the greeting *shavu'a tov*—'have a good week'; on the Jewish New Year you will hear *shanah tovah*—'good New Year'; and during the other Jewish holidays you may hear the greeting *mo'adim lesimḥah*—'happy holiday.'

Addressing people

If you know the person by name, address him as *mar Cohen*, using his surname—or *adon Cohen*; address a woman as *geveret*. If you know the person on a first-name basis, address him or her by his or her first name: *Shalom Ya'akov. Mah shlomcha?* You may address a stranger as 'sir'—*adoni*, and a woman as *gevirti* (pronounced *gvirtí*)—madam.

Saying 'please' and 'thank you'

Bevakashah	Please—when you want something, or to draw someone's attention. It may be used by a clerk in a store, bank, or hotel to inquire how he may help you.
Todah	Thank (you)—for something you've been given or offered. When you decline the offer, say: *lo, todah.*
Todah rabah	Many thanks—when you want to express your deep gratitude.

Food and drink

The bigger hotels have restaurants and bars; a few include a 'continental breakfast' (toast, butter, jam and coffee) in the quoted price for a room. You may order your room on a 'half-board' basis, which includes room and breakfast plus one meal, or 'full board'—all meals included. A 'full breakfast,' referred to also as an 'Israeli breakfast,' is a buffet-style feast in itself, including all kinds of cheeses, yogurts, fish and omelettes. Continental breakfast at a five-star hotel costs about $4.50, compared to the full-scale Israeli breakfast, which costs about $8. If you charge your meals to your room, you're exempted from the value added tax (VAT) of 15%, although you still have to pay 15% service charge. Paying cash will prove to be more costly, as you'll have to pay the VAT too. If you plan to stay at your hotel on the Sabbath, order your meals in advance.

For those who would like to try new and exotic food, there is a variety of *misadot* (restaurants) specializing in all sorts of cuisines. For more details, see Unit Five. For a quick drink you may go to one of the many *kiosks* (snack bars) or to a *beit kafe* (a café, or coffee shop).

For a hot drink you can order *tei im limon* (tea with lemon) or *tei im ḥalav* (tea with milk), or a variety of coffees:

Kafe shaḥor	Regular black coffee
Kafe im ḥalav	Regular coffee with milk
Nes kafe	Instant coffee, with or without milk
Kafe turki	Special coffee, boiled to form aromatic foam, served in a small cup
Espresso	European espresso coffee or capuccino, where fluffed boiling milk is added to the coffee

Rate of exchange

With the current high inflation (190% per year) in Israel, the rate of exchange fluctuates almost daily, and so do prices. Prices used in this book and tapes are for practice only and do not reflect actual prices. Check the going rate of exchange before you change your foreign currency at the hotel. They usually charge more than the banks for the service. The banks, of course, will give you the current rate.

2 Getting a hotel room

Listen to some of the words which you are about to hear in this unit, trying to get used to the sound of Hebrew. Watch out for some familiar words.

Desk clerk Yesh lanu ḥeder panuy
יש לנו חדר פנוי
lezug, im mitah kefulah,
לזוג, עם מיטה כפולה,
sherutim, televizyah,
שירותים, טלוויזיה,
mirpeset, kolel
מירפסת, כולל
aruḥat boker.
ארוחת בוקר.

Have you done the assignment from Unit One?

You Melt́zar! Śendvitch, bevakaśhah!
מלצר! סנדוויץ׳ בבקשה!

Waiter Śandvich eḥ́ad bishv́il ha'ad́on.
Mah tisht́eh?
סנדוויץ׳ אחד בשביל האדון.
מה תשתה?

You B́irah, bevakaśhah.
בירה, בבקשה.

Key words and phrases

Mah uchal . . . ?	What can I . . . ?
La'asot bishvilcha	(To) do for you
Bemah uchal . . . ?	With what (how) can I . . . ?
La'azor lecha	(To) help you
Yesh lachem?	(Do) you (m. pl.) have?
Ḥeder panuy	A vacant room
Yesh lanu	We have
Lelaylah	For a night

Booking a hotel room

Desk clerk	Ken, bevakaśhah?	כן, בבקשה?
	or	
Desk clerk	Mah ućhal la'aśot bishvilćha?	מה אוכל לעשות בשבילך?
	or	
Desk clerk	Beḿah ućhal la'aźor lećha?	במה אוכל לעזור לך?
Guest	Yesh laćhem ḥeder pańuy?	יש לכם חדר פנוי?
Desk clerk	Ken. Yesh ĺanu ḥeder pańuy.	כן. יש לנו חדר פנוי.
Guest	Yesh laćhem ḥeder pańuy leĺaylah?	יש לכם חדר פנוי ללילה?
Desk clerk	Ken. Yesh ĺanu ḥeder pańuy leĺaylah.	כן. יש לנו חדר פנוי ללילה.

Key words and phrases

Lezug o leyaḥid?	For a couple (double) or (for a) single?
Im mitah kefulah	With a double bed
Sherutim	Conveniences; private bath and toilet
Mirpeset	Terrace, balcony
Kolel	Including
Aruḥat boker	Breakfast
Bishvil	For
Ha'adon	The gentleman
Vehageveret	And the Mrs., the lady
Ḥeder eḥad	One room
Lelaylah eḥad	For one night

What kind of accommodations?

Guest Érev tov.
ערב טוב.

Desk clerk Érev tov.
ערב טוב.

Guest Ḥeder, bevakaśhah.
חדר, בבקשה.

Desk clerk Ḥ́eder leźug o leyaḥ́id?
חדר לזוג או ליחיד?

Guest Ḥ́eder leźug.
חדר לזוג.

Desk clerk Yesh ĺanu ḥ́eder pańuy leźug, im mítah kefuĺah, sherutím, televízyah, mirṕeset, kóĺel aruḥat bóker.
יש לנו חדר פנוי לזוג ,עם
מיטה כפולה, שירותים, טלוויזיה,
מירפסת, כולל ארוחת בוקר.

Guest Metzuýan!
מצויין!

Desk clerk Ḥ́eder eḥ́ad bishvíl ha'adón vehageýeret!
חדר אחד בשביל
האדון והגברת!

or

Desk clerk Ḥ́eder leĺaylah eḥ́ad bishvíl ha'adón vehageýeret!
חדר ללילה אחד בשביל
האדון והגברת!

Key words and phrases

Lechamah?	For how many?
Shloshah leilot	Three nights
Yamim	Days
Mah hashem?	What is the name?
Mah shimcha?	What's your name? (to a male)
Mah schmech?	What's your name? (to a female)

Kamah zeh oleh?	How much does it cost? How much is it?
Ḥamishim vaḥamishah	Fifty-five
Shivim vaḥamishah	Seventy-five
Mafte'aḥ	Key
Hamafte'aḥ	The key
Shloshim ve'arba	Thirty-four

Booking a room for more than one night

Guest — B́oker tov. Yesh laćhem ḥeder pańuy?
בוקר טוב. יש לכם חדר פנוי?

Desk clerk — Lećhamah leiĺot?
לכמה לילות?

Guest — Shlośhah leiĺot.
שלושה לילות.

Desk clerk — Lećhamah yamim?
לכמה ימים?

Guest — Shlośhah yamim.
שלושה ימים.

Checking in

Desk clerk — Mah haśhem, bevakaśhah?
מה השם, בבקשה?

or

Desk clerk — Mah shimćha, bevakaśhah?
מה שִׁמְךָ, בבקשה?

Guest — Brown. Mar Yósef Brown.
בּראון. מר יוסף בּראון

Desk clerk — Mah shem hageveret?
מה שם הגברת?

Guest (m) — Shem hageveret Śarah; Śarah Brown.
שם הגברת שרה; שרה בּראון.

Desk clerk — Ḿah shmech?
מה שמֵךְ?

Guest (f) — Sarah Brown.
שרה בּראון

Asking the price

Guest — Ḱamah zeh oĺeh?

כמה זה עולה?

Desk clerk — Ḥ́eder leĺaylah leyaḥ́id oĺeh ḥamiśhim vaḥamiśhah d́ollar.

חדר ללילה ליחיד עולה
חמישים וחמישה דולר.

Guest — Ḱamah oĺeh ḥeder leźug?

כמה עולה חדר לזוג?

Desk clerk — Ḥ́eder leźug leĺaylah eḥ́ad oĺeh shiv́im vaḥamiśhah d́ollar.

חדר לזוג ללילה אחד
עולה שבעים וחמישה דולר

Asking for the key

Guest — Maft́e'aḥ, bevakaśhah.

מפתח, בבקשה.

Desk clerk — Ken, hamaft́e'aḥ . . . Maft́e'aḥ leḥ́eder shlośhim ve'árba.

כן, המפתח . . . מפתח
לחדר שלושים וארבע.

Guest — Maft́e'aḥ leḥ́eder shlośhim ve'árba.

מפתח לחדר שלושים וארבע.

Key words and phrases

Kan	Here (is)
Medaber	Speaks
Efshar	It is possible; (I) can; (I) may; *or* (as question): Is it possible?
Ledaber	To speak
Rega	A moment; (wait) a minute
Tafus	Busy
Panuy	Unoccupied, free
Hu	He
Nimtza	Be, is
Lo nimtza kan	Is not here
Hayom	Today (the day)
Titkasher	You should call, call
Maḥar	Tomorrow

Answering the phone . . .

Tourist	(*answering phone*) Haĺo.
	הלו.
Friend	Haĺo. Mar Rósen? Shaĺom. Kan mar Ćohen. Mah shlomćha?
	הלו. מר רוזן? שלום. כאן מר כהן. מה שלומד?
Tourist	Tov, todáh.
	טוב, תודה.
	or
Friend	Haĺo. Mar Rósen? Shaĺom. Medaber mar Ćohen. Mah shlomćha?
	הלו. מר רוזן? שלום. מדבר מר כהן. מה שלומך?

Tourist — Tov me'ód, tod́ah. Umah shlomćha, mar Ćohen?

טוב מאוד, תודה. ומה שלומך,
מר כהן?

Friend — Haḱol beśeder, tod́ah.

הכול בסדר, תודה.

Tourist — Beḿah ućhal la'aźor lećha?

במה אוכל לעזור לך?

or

Efśhar la'aźor lećha?

אפשר לעזור לך?

Friend — Efśhar ledab́er im gev́eret Rósen?

אפשר לדבר עם גברת רוזן?

Tourist — Ŕega, bevakaśhah.

רגע, בבקשה.

. . . and making a call

Man	(*dialing; busy signal*) Tafus! תפוס!
Man	(*dialing again; ringing*) Pañuy! פנוי!
Man	Halo. Kan mar Rośen. Efśhar ledaber im mar Brown? הלו. כאן מר רוזן. אפשר לדבר עם מר בראון?
Receptionist	Hu lo nimtza kan hayom. Titkaśher maḥar, bevakaśhah. הוא לא נמצא כאן היום. תתקשר מחר, בבקשה.

Key words and phrases

Sliḥah	Excuse me, pardon
Mah hasha'ah?	What is the time?
Hasha'ah shalosh	It is three o'clock
Hasha'ah arba	It is four o'clock
Tesha	Nine
Baboker	In the morning
Ad	Till, to
Aḥat	One
Aḥarei hatzohorayim	(In) the afternoon
Sheva	Seven
Ba'erev	In the evening
Hasha'ah shmoneh vaḥetzi	The time is half past eight (eight and a half)

Hasha'ah shmoneh ushloshim	The time is eight thirty
Hasha'ah tesha vareva	The time is a quarter past nine (nine and a quarter)
Hasha'ah reva aḥarei tesha	The time is a quarter past nine
Hasha'ah reva letesha	The time is a quarter to nine

Asking for the time

Tourist Sliḥah, mah hasha'áh, bevakaśhah?
סליחה, מה השעה בבקשה?

Stranger Hasha'áh shaĺosh.
השעה שלוש.

Tourist Mah hasha'áh, bevakaśhah?
מה השעה, בבקשה?

Stranger Hasha'áh arba.
השעה ארבע.

Being told when banks are open

Clerk Mi shmońeh vaḥétzi ad shteim esŕeh vaḥétzi aḥarei hatzohorayim. Miárba aḥarei hatzohorayim ad sheva ba'erev.
משמובה וחצי בבוקר עד שתים עשרה וחצי אחרי הצהריים. מארבע אחרי הצהריים עד שבע בערב.

Listening to the wake-up call

Tourist (*answering phone*) Haĺo?
הלו?

Operator B́oker tov. Hasha'áh shḿoneh vaḥetzi.
בוקר טוב. השעה שמונה וחצי.

Tourist Haĺo?
הלו?

Operator B́oker tov. Hasha'áh t́esha vaŕeva.
בוקר טוב. השעה תשע ורבע.

or

Hasha'áh ŕeva aḥaŕei t́esha.
השעה רבע אחרי תשע.

Tourist <u>Haĺo</u>?

הלו?

Operator B́oker tov. Hasha'áh ŕeva let́esha.

בוקר טוב. השעה רבע לתשע.

Telling time

7:30 am śheva vaḥ́etzi bab́oker

שבע וחצי בבוקר

2:15 pm sht́ayim vaŕeva aḥaŕei hat́zohoŕayim

שתיים ורבע אחרי הצהריים

5:45 pm ŕeva leśhesh ba'érev

רבע לשש בערב

10:30 pm éser ushlośhim baĺaylah

עשר ושלושים בלילה

11:00 pm hasha'áh aḥ́at esŕeh baĺaylah

השעה אחת עשרה בלילה

12:00 hasha'áh sht́eim esŕeh

השעה שתים עשרה

midnight ḥat́zot
achśhav ḥat́zot

חצות
עכשיו חצות

Assignment for next time

Think of how to say 'ten past the hour, twenty, forty, and fifty minutes past the hour.' You may wish to review numbers one to ten and Telling Time in this unit, and the additional section on numbers in Unit Three.

Language summary

What you need to say

Booking a hotel room

Yesh lachem ḥeder panuy lelaylah?	*a room for one night*
Ḥeder, bevakashah	*asking for a room*
Ḥeder lezug	*a double room*

Asking the price
Kamah zeh oleh?
Kamah oleh ḥeder lezug?

Asking for the key
Mafte'aḥ, bevakashah

Making a call
Kan mar Rosen

identifying yourself

Asking for the time
Sliḥah, mah hasha'ah, bevakashah?

Just a minute!
Rega, bevakashah

What you need to listen for

Being asked what you want
Ken, bevakashah?
Mah uchal la'asot bishvilcha?

Being told there's a room
Ken. Yesh lanu ḥeder panuy lelaylah

Being asked for your name
Mah hashem, bevakashah?
Mah shimcha, bevakashah? (m.)
Mah shmech, bevakashah? (f.)

Being told kind of accommodations
Ḥeder lezug o leyaḥid?
Yesh lanu ḥeder panuy lezug
Ḥeder lelaylah eḥad
Lechamah leilot?

Explanations

And

The conjunction 'and' is *ve*; it is placed at the beginning of a word: *ve'arba* (and four). When used with the definite article, it precedes it: *vehageveret*. Occasionally it is changed to *va*, as in *vaḥetzi*, or *vaḥamishah*, *vaḥamishim, vareva.* Before certain consonants (B, V, M, P), it changes to *u,* as in *umah* (and what). Most Israelis will not observe the grammatical changes from *ve* to *va* and *u,* and will say *veḥamishah* and *vemah.*

Plural

The plural is formed by adding the ending *im* for the masculine:

ḥeder	ḥadarim
shekel	shkalim

For the feminine, the *ah* ending changes to *ot*:

ugah	ugot
sha'ah	sha'ot

As you may have noticed, some nouns undergo slight changes in their plural forms besides the endings: *ḥeder, ḥadarim.* But don't worry if you mispronounce them. People will understand you anyway.

Verbs

The future tense in spoken Hebrew may substitute for an imperative (command): *titkasher*—'you should call.' Regular future verb: *tishteh*—'you will drink.'

Pronouns

	Singular			Plural		
Masc.	*ani*	I	אני	aṅaḥnu	we	אנחנו
	atah	you	אתה	atem	you	אתם
	hu	he	הוא	hem	they	הם
Fem.	*ani*	I	אני	aṅaḥnu	we	אנחנו
	at	you	את	aten	you	אתן
	hi	she	היא	hen	they	הן

Numbers

Numbers also come in masculine and feminine forms:

	Feminine	*Masculine*			
1	aḥat	eḥad	אחד	אחת	1
2	shtayim	shnayim	שניים	שתיים	2
	(shtei)	(shnei)	(שני)	(שתי)	

	Feminine	Masculine			
3	shaĺosh	shlośhah	שלושה	שלוש	3
4	árba	arba'áh	ארבעה	ארבע	4
5	ḥaḿesh	ḥamiśhah	חמישה	חמש	5
6	śhesh	shiśhah	שישה	שש	6
7	śheva	shiv́ah	שבעה	שבע	7
8	shḿoneh	shmońah	שמונָה	שמונֶה	8
9	t́esha	tisháh	תשעה	תשע	9
10	éser	asaŕah	עשרה	עשר	10

When counting, use the feminine form: *aḥat,* shtayim, *shalosh* . . . (one, two, three . . .). Unfortunately, the rule for masculine and feminine endings is the reverse for numbers: *ah* indicates the *masculine.* Numbers come before the words they describe and agree with them in gender:

shishah duvdevanim (m. pl.)
shesh sha'ot (f. pl.)
shloshah shkalim (m. pl.)
shalosh ugot (f. pl.)

The number 'one' is an exception. It always follows the word it describes:

ḥeder *eḥad* (m. sing.)
birah *aḥat* (f. sing.)

The number 'two' (*shnayim*) is shortened to *shnei* in the masculine and *shtei* in the feminine: *shnei ḥadarim; shtei ugot.*

Telling time

You tell time in Hebrew using the feminine numbers with *hasha'ah* (the hour): *hasha'ah aḥat* (one o'clock).

The definite article *ha* is used also in the following 'timely' expressions:

haýom	today	היום
haĺaylah	tonight	הלילה
h́a'érev	this evening	הערב
hashańah	this year	השנה

Other expressions of time are:

etḿol	yesterday	אתמול
maḥ́ar	tomorrow	מחר
lifńei hatzohoŕayim	before noon	לפני הצהריים

Notes on accents

Accent marks are used here according to the *spoken* Hebrew, which is different from formal Hebrew. Thus we say *éifo* rather than *eifó, shmóneh* rather than *shmonéh, árba* rather than *arbá.*

Worth knowing

Hotel accommodations

Hotels in Israel are classified from the top-grade five stars (*****) down to one star (*). Some of the most luxurious modern hotels may be found in Tel Aviv, Jerusalem, Haifa, and Elat, and near the Dead Sea. During the tourist season (summer; high holidays, in September and October; Passover, around April; and, in Jerusalem, Christmas), it is recommended to make reservations in advance. If you don't have reservations, you can inquire about available rooms at the tourist information booth at the airport. Hotel rates are given in U.S. dollars, to which a 15% service charge is added. If you pay with foreign currency, you'll be exempt from the additional 15% value added tax and some other taxes. A few hotels include a continental breakfast in the price, although you may book your room on a half- or full-board basis (see Unit One).

Using the telephone

The hotel will add a surcharge for any calls you dial directly or make through the hotel operator. If you want to use public phones, you'll have to get tokens (*asimonim*), usually at the post office or at any of the shops that sell stamps. These shops will have a blue sign with a deer,—symbol of the Israeli Post Office—indicating that they are authorized to sell stamps and telephone tokens. Since the *asimonim* are cheap, the post offices and shops run out of them quickly. It is best to get them early in the morning. To make a long-distance call, place a few *asimonim* in the telephone slot (you can see them being 'swallowed' very fast!) Make sure that there is always an *asimon* inside; otherwise your call will automatically be cut off. Learn to distinguish the particular signals for busy' and 'ringing,' which are different from the ones you are used to in the U.S. To make long-distance (between cities) calls, you'll have to dial the area code:

Jerusalem	02
Tel Aviv	03
Haifa	04
Beer Sheva	057

Before making a call, read the directions posted on the phone.

Some important telephone numbers

information	14	Magen David Adom (first aid)	101
correct time	15	police	100
sending cables	171	fire department	102
wake-up calls	19		
international calls	18		

Business hours

banks	8:30 am to 12:30; 4:00 to 5:30 pm Sunday through Thursday; Wednesday and Friday 8:30 am to 12 noon. Some banks are now open until 6 pm daily and to 12:30 pm on Wednesdays and Fridays.
government offices	open to the public 8:30 am to 12:30 pm Sunday to Thursday
stores and shops	8:30 am to 1:00 pm; 4:00 to 7:00 pm Sunday to Thursday; Friday 8:30 am to 1:00 pm

Most stores have half-day schedules on Tuesdays. Some stores and markets are open continuously throughout the day. Days preceding Jewish holidays have a Friday schedule. Learn to distinguish between the Hebrew characters for the signs 'open'—*patu'aḥ*: פתוח, and 'closed'—*sagur*: סגור.

3 Getting your shopping done

Listen to a sample of the sentences which you will learn in this unit, trying to understand what they mean from the context, the situation they seem to portray, and from some familiar words both in Hebrew and in English. Try to place familiar phrases in the new setting.

At the kiosk

Customer Ɓoker tov.

בוקר טוב.

Seller Ɓoker tov.

בוקר טוב.

Customer Efŝhar lekaɓel siǵaryot?

אפשר לקבל סיגריות?

Seller Aťah roťzeh siǵaryot im ﬁlter o bli ﬁlter?

אתה רוצה סיגריות עם פילטר
או בלי פילטר?

Customer Im ﬁlter, bevakaŝhah.

עם פילטר, בבקשה.

Seller Siǵaryot Bŕodvey, Taym, Ṕarlament, o Kent?

סיגריות ברודווי, טיים, פארלאמנט,
או קנט?

Customer Bŕodvey, bevakaŝhah.

ברודווי, בבקשה.

Have you done the assignment from Unit Two?

Before doing the assignment you may wish to consult the sections on numbers and telling time in Unit Two, and the additional section on numbers later on in this unit.

Tell the time in Hebrew

4:10 Árba va'asaŕah ארבע ועשרה

6:20	śhesh ve'esŕim	שש ועשרים
7:30	śheva ushlośhim	שבע ושלושים
8:40	shḿoneh ve'arba'ím	שמונֶה וארבעים
	or	
	esŕim let́esha	עשרים לתשע
8:50	shḿoneh vaḥamiśhim	שמונֶה וחמישים
	or	
	asaŕah let́esha	עשרה לתשע
10:15	ŕeva aḥaŕei éser	רבע אחרי עשר
	or	
	éser vaŕeva	עשר ורבע
10:45	ŕeva le'aḥ́at esŕeh	רבע לאחת עשרה
	or	
	éser arba'ím veḥaḿesh	עשר ארבעים וחמש
12:30 am	sht́eim esŕeh vaḥ́etzi baĺaylah	שתים עשרה וחצי בלילה
	or	
	sht́eim esŕeh ushĺośhim aḥaŕei ḥat́zot	שתים עשרה ושלושים אחרי חצות

Key words and phrases

Eifo?	Where?
Sham	There
Ein li	I don't have
Lehamir	To convert, exchange
Hamḥa'ot nose'im	Travelers checks
Laḥtom	To sign
Taḥtom	You'll sign; sign (imperative)
Mitzta'er	Sorry; I am sorry
Kamah oleh (m.) **Kamah olah (f.)**	How much? What is the price of . . . ?
Kamah zeh oleh?	How much does this cost?
Kamah zeh?	How much is it?
Esrim vaḥamishah shkalim	25 shekels
Kolel mas erech musaf	Including value added tax
Kabel odef	Accept change
Ḥamishim	Fifty

At the bank

Customer Efśhar lehaḥaĺif ḱesef?

אפשר להחליף כסף?

or

Customer Éifo efśhar lehaḥaĺif ḱesef?

איפה אפשר להחליף כסף?

Teller Sham!

שם!

. . . changing money

Teller At́ah rot́zeh lehaḥaĺif doĺarim?

אתה רוצה להחליף דולרים?

Customer	Ken, yesh li doĺarim.	כן, יש לי דולרים.
	or	
Customer	Efśhar lehaḥaĺif ḱesef?	אפשר להחליף כסף?
Teller	Aťah roťzeh lehaḿir doĺarim?	אתה רוצה להמיר דולרים?
Customer	Ken, yesh li doĺarim.	כן, יש לי דולרים.
Teller	Yesh lećúha ťravelers cheks?	יש לך טרוולרס צ׳קס?
	or	
Teller	Yesh lećha hamḥa'ót nos'ím?	יש לך המחאות נוסעים?
Customer	Ken.	כן.
Teller	Passṕort, bevakaśhah. Bevakaśhah laḥťom!	פספורט, בבקשה. בבקשה לחתום!
Teller	Passṕort, bevakaśhah. Taḥťom, bevakaśhah!	פספורט, בבקשה. תחתום בבקשה!

Getting a newspaper at the kiosk

Customer	*Jeŕusalem Post*, bevakaśhah.	*ג׳רוזאלם פוסט*, בבקשה.
	or	
Customer	Et ha-*Jeŕusalem Post*, bevakaśhah.	את הג׳*רוזאלם פוסט*, בבקשה.
Seller	Mitzta'ér. Ein li *Jeŕusalem Post.*	מצטער. אין לי *ג׳רוזאלם פוסט*.
Customer	Et ha-*Ḣerald Ťribune*, bevakaśhah.	את ה*הרלד טריביון*, בבקשה.
Seller	Mitzta'ér. Ein li Ḣerald Ťribune.	מצטער. אין לי *הרלד טריביון*.

Asking for the price

Customer Ḱamah oĺeh ha-*Jeŕusalem Post*?

כמה עולה הג׳רוזאלם פוסט?

Seller Esŕim vaḥamiśhah shkaĺim,
koĺel mas érech muśaf.

עשרים וחמישה שקלים,
כולל מס ערך מוסף.

Customer Ḱamah oĺeh haḥeder?

כמה עולה החדר?

Customer Ḱamah oĺeh kaf́e?

כמה עולה קפה?

Customer Ḱamah oĺah aruḥ́at b́oker?

כמה עוֹלָה ארוחת בוקר?

Customer Ḱamah zeh oĺeh?

כמה זה עולה?

Customer Ḱamah zeh?

כמה זה?

. . . and paying

Customer Ḱamah zeh oĺeh?

כמה זה עולה?

Seller Ḥamiśhim shkaĺim.

חמישים שקלים.

Customer Bevakaśhah.

בבקשה.

Getting some change

Seller (*Receiving a 100-shekel note:*)
Ḥamiśhim shkaĺim. Kab́el ódef
ḥamiśhim shkaĺim.

חמישים שקלים. קבל עודף
חמישים שקלים.

Key words and phrases

Sigaryot Cigarettes
Im filter With a filter
Bli filter Without a filter

Eizeh (m.)	Which
Et zeh	This
Esrim	Twenty
Agorot	100 agorot in a shekel
Todah rabah	Many thanks (much thanks)

Getting cigarettes

Customer Efśhar lekaber siǵaryot?
אפשר לקבל סיגריות?
or

Customer Yesh lećha siǵaryot?
יש לך סיגריות?

Seller Aťah roťzeh siǵaryot im ḟilter
o bli ḟilter?
אתה רוצה סיגריות עם פילטר
או בלי פילטר?

Customer Siǵaryot im ḟilter, bevakaśhah.
סיגריות עם פילטר, בבקשה.
or

Customer Siǵaryot bli ḟilter, bevakaśhah.
סיגריות בלי פילטר, בבקשה.

Seller Éizeh siǵaryot aťah roťzeh?
Bŕodvey, Taym, Ṕarlament, o Kent?
איזה סיגריות אתה רוצה?
ברודווי, טיים, פארלאמנט, או קנט?

Customer Bŕodvey, bevakaśhah.
ברודווי, בבקשה.

Ordering this and that . . .

Customer Et zeh, bevakaśhah.
את זה, בבקשה.

Customer Ḱamah zeh oĺeh?
כמה זה עולה?

Seller Esŕim shkaĺim ve'esŕim agoŕot.
עשרים שקלים ועשרים אגורות.

. . . and saying 'thank you' differently

Customer Toďah raḃah.
תודה רבה.

Key words and phrases

Asimonim	Tokens
Shmona asar	Eighteen
Bulim	Stamps
Ba'aretz	In the land (domestic)
Leḥutz la'aretz	To countries outside of Israel (abroad)
Le'amerika	To America (The U.S.)
Bulei	Stamps of
Do'ar avir	Airmail
Lemichtav	For a letter
Ligluyah	For a postcard
Lechamah?	For how many?
Shloshim ushnayim vaḥetzi	Thirty-two and a half
Beyaḥad	Together (total)
Rak rega	Just a minute
Arba'im vetish'ah vaḥetzi	Forty-nine and a half
Me'ah	One hundred

At the post office

Customer Efśhar lekabél <u>asimońim</u>?
אפשר לקבל אסימונים?

Clerk	Ken. Ḱamah aťah roťzeh? כן. כמה אתה רוצה?
Customer	Asaŕah asimońim, bevakaśhah. Ḱamah zeh oĺeh? עשרה אסימונים, בבקשה. כמה זה עולה?
Clerk	Shmońah aśar shkaĺim. שמונה עשר שקלים.
Customer	Yesh lećha buĺim? יש לך בולים?
Clerk	Ken. Ba'áretz o leḣutz la'áretz? כן. בארץ או לחוץ לארץ?
Customer	Buĺim leḣutz la'áretz; le'aḿerika. בולים לחוץ לארץ; לאמריקה.
Clerk	Buĺei ďo'ar aví́r? בולי דואר אוויר?
Customer	Ken. כן.
Clerk	Lemichťav o ligluýah? למיכתב או לגלוידה?
Customer	Buĺim ligluýah. בולים לגלוידה.
Clerk	Lećhamah gluyot? לכמה גלויות?
Customer	Leḣaḿesh gluýot. לחמש גלויות.
Clerk	Bevakaśhah. בבקשה.
Customer	Ḱamah zeh óleh? כמה זה עולה?
Clerk	Rak ŕega . . . Habuĺim—shlośhim ushńayim vaḣetzi shkalim. Veha'asimońim—shmońah aśar. Beýaḥad: ḥamiśhim shkaĺim vaḥamiśhim agorot. רק רגע . . . הבולים – שלושים ושניים וחצי שקלים. והאסימונים – שמונה עשר ביחד: חמישים שקלים וחמישים אגורות.
Customer	Bevakaśhah me'áh shkaĺim. בבקשה מאה שקלים.

Clerk Kabél ódef arbaím vetish'áh vaḥétzi shkalím.

קַבֵּל עודף ארבעים ותשעה וחצי שקלים.

Customer Tódah rabáh.

תודה רבה.

Key words and phrases

Mish'ḥat shinayim	Toothpaste
Ten li	Give me; let me have
Eizo? (f.)	Which one?
Gedolah (f.)	Large
Ketanah (f.)	Small
Mivreshet shinayim	Toothbrush
Rakah (f.)	Soft
Kashah (f.)	Hard
Ḥafisat aspirin	A packet (pack) of aspirin

At the drugstore

Customer Shalóm.

שלום.

Pharmacist Shalóm. Baméh uchál la'azór lecha?

שלום. במה אוּכל לַעזור לךָ?

Customer Efshar lekabél mish'ḥat shinayim?

אפשר לקַבֵּל מִשחת שִׁניים?

or

Customer Yesh lecha mish'ḥat shinayim?

יש לךָ מִשחת שִׁניים?

or

Customer Ten li bevakashah mish'ḥat shinayim.

תן לי בבקשה מִשחת שִׁניים.

Pharmacist Eizo mish'ḥat shinayim atáh rotzéh? Gedoláh o ketanáh?

איזו מִשחת שִׁניים אתה רוצה?
גדולה או קטנה?

Customer Ten li mish'ḥat shińayim ketańah.

תן לי מִשחת שִׁניים קטנה.

or

Customer Ten li mish'ḥat shińayim gedoĺah.

תן לי מִשחת שִׁניים גדולה.

Customer . . . mivŕeshet shińayim . . .

. . . מברשת שניים . . .

Pharmacist At́ah rot́zeh mivŕeshet shińayim raḱah o kaśhah?

אתה רוצה מִברשת שִׁניים רכּה או קשה?

Customer Mivŕeshet shińayim raḱah.

מִברשת שִׁניים רכּה.

or

Customer Ten li mivŕeshet raḱah.

תן לי מִברשת רכּה.

Customer . . . ve'aspiŕin.

. . . ואספירין.

Pharmacist Ḥafiśat aspiŕin ketańah o gedoĺah?

חפיסת אספירין קטנה או גדולה?

Customer Ḥafiśat aspiŕin ketańah, bevakaśhah.

חפיסת אספירין קטנה, בבקשה.

Key words and phrases

Leḥem	Bread
Lavan (m.)	White
Ḥetzi	A half
Kikar	Loaf
Sakit	(Soft plastic) container
Agvaniyot	Tomatoes
Melafefonim	Cucumbers
Tapuzim	Oranges
Vechama	And a few
Bananot	Bananas

Grocery shopping

Customer	Ten li léḥem, bevakaśhah. תן לי לחם, בבקשה.
Grocer	Léḥem shaḥor o laván? לחם שחור או לבן?
Customer	Léḥem laván. לחם לבן.
Customer	Ḥétzi, bevakaśhah. חֵצי, בבקשה. *or*
Customer	Ḥatzi léḥem laván, bevakaśhah. חַצי לחם לבן,בבקשה. *or*
Customer	Ḥatzi kikar léḥem laván, bevakaśhah. חֲצי כיכר לחם לבן, בבקשה.
Customer	Ḥalav katan, bevakaśhah. חלב קטן, בבקשה. *or*
Customer	Ḥalav besakit gedolah, bevakaśhah. חלב בשקית גדולה, בבקשה.
Customer	Ten li kilo agvaniýot, shńayim o shlośhah melafefońim, kilo tapuḥim, shńei kilo tapuźim, većhamah bańanot. תן לי קילו עגבניות, שניים או שלושה מלפפונים, קילו תפוחים, שני קילו תפוזים, וכמה בננות.
Customer	Kamah zeh oleh? כמה זה עולה?
Customer	Todah rabah. תודה רבה.

Key words and phrases

Anglit	English
Ivrit	Hebrew

Ktzat	A little
At (f. sing.)	You
Medaberet (f. sing.)	Speak(s)
Yidish	Yiddish

Asking 'do you speak English?' (and other languages)

Customer Aťah medaber anglit?
אתה מדבר אנגלית?

Attendant Aťah medaber ivŕit?
אתה מדבר עברית?

Customer Ktzat!
קצת!

Customer At medaberet anglit?
אַתְּ מדַבֶּרת אנגלית?

Attendant Ken. Ani medaberet anglit.
כן. אני מדַבֶּרת אנגלית.

Customer At medaberet ýidish?
אַתְּ מדברת אידיש?

Attendant Lo.
לא.

Key words and phrases

Taḥanat hadelek	The gas station.
Male!	Fill (it up)!
Delek	Fuel, gas
Benzin tishim ve'eḥad	91-octane gas
Benzin tishim ve'arba'ah	High octane, 94-octane gas
Baḥamesh me'ot	At (for) five hundred
Ten li	Let me have; give me
Esrim liter	Twenty liters

Asking where the gas station is

Driver Éifo taḥańat hadelek?
איפה תחנת הדלק?

Getting gas

Driver	Malé, bevakaśhah! מלֵא, בבקשה!
Attendant	Éizeh ́delek, bevakaśhah? איזה דלק, בבקשה?
Driver	Benźin tishím ve'eḥad, bevakaśhah. בנזין תשעים ואחד, בבקשה.
	or
Driver	Benźin tishím ve'árba'ah. בנזין תשעים וארבעה.

. . . and other ways of ordering gas

Driver	Ďelek baḥaḿesh me'ót śhekel, bevakaśhah. דלק בחמש מאות שקל, בבקשה.
	or
Driver	Benźin tishím ve'eḥad baḥamesh me'ót śhekel, bevakaśhah. בנזין תשעים ואחד בחמש מאות שקל, בבקשה.
	or
Driver	Ten li esŕim ĺiter benźin tishím ve'eḥad. תן לי עשרים ליטר בנזין תשעים ואחד.

Key words and phrases

Tivdok	Check
Hamayim	The water
Haradiator	The radiator
Bemayim	With water
Hashemen	The oil
Ha'avir	The air
Hakol beseder gamur	Everything is absolutely O.K.
Hamusach	The garage

Hagaraj	The garage
Patu'aḥ (m.)	Open
Lo patu'aḥ	Not open
Sagur (m.)	Closed
Mashehu lo beseder	Something is wrong
Im hamechonit	With the car

Getting your car checked

Driver Tivdók bevakaśhah et hamáyim.
תבדוק בבקשה את המים.

Driver Tivdók et haradíator bevakaśhah.
תבדוק את הראדיאטור בבקשה.

Driver Malé et haradíator bemáyim, bevakaśhah.
מלא את הראדיאטור במים, בבקשה.

Attendant Haradíator beśeder!
הראדיאטור בסדר!

Driver Tivdók bevakaśhah et haśhemen.
תבדוק בבקשה את השמן.

Attendant Haśhemen beśeder!
השמן בסדר!

Driver Tivdók bevakaśhah et ha'avír.
תבדוק בבקשה את האוויר.

Attendant Hakól beśeder gamúr!
הכול בסדר גמור!

. . . and serviced at the garage

Driver Hamuśach patú'aḥ?
המוסך פתוח?

or

Driver Hagaráj patú'aḥ?
הגרז' פתוח?

Attendant Ken, patú'aḥ.
כן, פתוח.

or

Attendant Lo. Hamuśach lo patú'aḥ. Hamuśach sagúr.
לא. המוסך לא פתוח. המוסך סגור.

Driver	Ḿashehu lo beśeder im hamechońit. משהו לא בסדר עם המכונית.

Assignment for next time

Think how to ask for directions to the bus station, and whether it is open or closed.

Language summary

What you need to say

Changing money at the bank

Efshar lehaḥalif kesef?
Eifo efshar lehaḥalif kesef?
Ken yesh li dolarim

Buying cigarettes

Efshar lekabel sigaryot?
Yesh lecha sigaryot?

I want this

Et zeh, bevakashah

Being grateful

Todah rabah

Getting stamps and 'asimonim'

Efshar lekabel asimonim?
Asarah asimonim, bevakashah
Yesh lecha bulim?
Bulim leḥutz la'aretz; le'amerika

At the pharmacy

Efshar lekabel mish'ḥat shinayim?
Yesh lecha mish'ḥat shinayim?
Ten li mivreshet shinayim
Ten li aspirin

Food shopping

Ten li leḥem, bevakashah
Ḥalav katan, bevakashah
Ḥalav besakit gedolah, bevakashah

Getting your car serviced

Eifo taḥanat hadelek?
Male, bevakashah!
Tivdok et haradiator, bevakashah
Tivdok bevakashah et ha'avir
Hagaraj patu'aḥ
Mashehu lo beseder

Tivdok bevakashah et hashemen

im hamechonit

What you need to listen for

Changing money

Atah rotzeh lehaḥalif dolarim?

Yesh lecha travelers cheks?
Bevakashah laḥtom!

Being told how much something costs

Ḥamishim shkalim

Kabel odef

Getting cigarettes

Atah rotzeh sigaryot im filter o bli filter?

At the post office

Ken. Kamah atah rotzeh?
Ken. Ba'aretz o leḥutz la'aretz?

Bulei do'ar avir?

Food shopping

Leḥem shaḥor o lavan?

On the move with your car

Eizeh delek, bevakashah?
Haradiator beseder!
Hashemen beseder!
Hakol beseder gamur!

Ken, hamusach patu'aḥ
Lo. Hamusach lo patu'aḥ
Hamusach sagur

Explanations

Of

mish'ḥat shinayim	a paste *of* teeth	toothpaste
bulei do'ar avir	stamps *of* airmail	airmail stamps
misredei hamemshalah	offices *of* the government	government offices
ugat gevinah	cake *of* cheese	cheese cake
aruḥat boker	meal *of* the morning	breakfast

In this form, when a word such as *ugah* is to be linked with another by the word *of*, as in *cake of cheese* or *cheese cake*, it changes to *ugat* meaning *cake of*—as in *ugat gevinah*, a cake of cheese. The ending *t* replaces the preposition *of*. The masculine plural ending *im* commonly changes to *ei: bulim—bulei;* and the feminine singular ending *ah* changes to *at: ugah—ugat.* However, there are many exceptions to this rule.

More about verbs

Like English, Hebrew often uses a command (the imperative form of the verb) to ask for something:

Ten li, bevakashah, mish'ḥat shinayim	*Give* me some toothpaste, please
Male!	*Fill* it up!
Kabel odef ḥamishim shkalim	*Take* your change of 50 shekels

Sometimes the future tense is used for the imperative:

Taḥtom, bevakashah	*Sign,* please
Tivdok, bevakashah, et hamayim	*Check* the water, please

More questions

Eifo efshar lehaḥalif kesef?	Where can I exchange money?
Eizeh sigaryot atah rotzeh?	Which cigarettes do you want?
Kamah zeh oleh?	How much is it?

Saying 'No'

The Hebrew word for 'no' or 'not is *lo:*

Lo yode'a (m.)	I don't know
Lo yoda'at (f.)	I don't know
Hamusach lo patu'aḥ	The garage is not open
Lo beseder	Not well

The negative form for *yesh li* (I have) is *ein li* (I don't have).

Numbers

	Feminine	Masculine	זכר	נקבה	
11	aḥat esŕeh	aḥad aśar	אחד עשר	אחת עשרה	11

12	sht́eim	shńeim	שנים	שתים	12
	eśŕeh	aśar	עשר	עשרה	
13	shĺosh	shlośhah	שלושה	שלוש	13
	esŕeh	aśar	עשר	עשרה	
14	arb́a	arba'áh	ארבעה	ארבע	14
	esŕeh	aśar	עשר	עשרה	
15	ḥaḿesh	ḥamiśhah	חמישה	חמש	15
	esŕeh	aśar	עשר	עשרה	
16	shesh	shiśhah	שישה	שש	16
	esŕeh	aśar	עשר	עשרה	
17	shva	shiváh	שבעה	שְבע	17
	esŕeh	aśar	עשר	עְשרה	
18	shmońeh	shmońah	שמונָה	שמונֶה	18
	esŕeh	aśar	עשר	עשרה	
19	teśha	tisháh	תשעה	תְשע	19
	esŕeh	aśar	עשר	עְשרה	

20	esŕim	עשרים
30	shlośhim	שלושים
40	arba'ím	ארבעים
50	ḥamiśhim	חמישים
60	shiśhim	שישים
70	shivím	שבעים
80	shmońim	שמונים
90	tishím	תשעים
100	me'áh	מאה
200	mat́ayim	מאתיים
300	shĺosh me'ót	שלוש מאות
400	arb́a me'ót	ארבע מאות
500	ḥaḿesh me'ót	חמש מאות
600	shesh me'ót	שש מאות
700	shva me'ót	שְבע מאות
800	shmońeh me'ót	שמונֶה מאות
900	teśha me'ót	תְשע מאות

The hundreds are formed by the single numbers in the feminine with the word *me'ot* (plural of *me'ah*, which is feminine). Thus *shalosh* becomes *shlosh me'ot*; *sheva* becomes *shva me'ot*; *tesha* becomes *tesha me'ot*.

Nouns following numbers eleven and up sometimes appear in the singular, especially following the hundreds, when applied to measurements and money. Thus: *esrim liter* (20 liters); *ḥamesh me'ot shekel* (500 shekels); *shesh me'ot shekel* (600 shekels). Nouns following numbers two to ten must be in the plural form: *shlosha ḥadarim* (three rooms); *arba bananot* (four bananas). For numbers above twenty-one, use 'and'—*ve, va,* or *u*:

35 shloshim veḥamesh (f.)
45 arba'im vaḥamishah (m.)
88 shmonim ushmonah (m.)
175 me'ah shivim vaḥamishah (m.)

Watch out!

Expressions in one language often cannot be translated literally into another. 'I don't have time' in Hebrew is *Ein li zman! The idiom Ma hasha'ah*, "What is the time?", literally means, "What is the hour?" So, don't say: *Ein li sha'ah* . . . And don't wish your friend 'a good time' by translating 'good time' from English. Instead, you should use the *equivalent* in Hebrew, and say: *Biluy na'im!* And we wish you too, *Biluy na'im!*

Worth knowing

Security check

Upon entering public places (museums, theaters, movie houses, etc.), you may be asked to have your briefcase or handbag checked. It is a common practice in Israel, resulting from its unique situation. You probably went through a more thorough check before you boarded the El Al plane.

Modi'in

Learn to say the word, 'modi'in,' so that you may be able to ask for it when you need *information*. Try to identify the word in Hebrew—מודיעין—in order to be able to find the sign by yourself. Many public places have *Lishkat Modi'in*—an information office. There are several tourist information offices in major cities, and one at the Ben Gurion International Airport. At the bank, ask one of the bank's officers or tellers what you need to know.

Changing money

Since some banks charge a set sum, or minimum, for changing travelers checks and foreign currencies, it is better at times to exchange higher denominations. You should keep some foreign currency with you for shops and stores that offer special discounts to tourists paying with foreign currency. You may also change money at the hotel's cashier, although the rate of exchange may not be as good as at the bank. In East Jerusalem you can find money changers who do not charge a bank's fee for the exchange.

Newspapers

Israel has a variety of newspapers in many languages, in addition to the Hebrew dailies and periodicals. The local English daily is *The Jerusalem Post.* Many international editions of European and American newspapers, weeklies, and journals are available at hotels and at English bookstores (such as Steimatzky's).

Bargaining

At the market and in many stores in the Old City of Jerusalem, as well as some other places, when given a price, bargaining is an acceptable practice.

Credit cards

All major credit cards are accepted in most tourist shops. Check with the shop manager whether your card is accepted.

Post office

Main branches are open continuously from 8 am to 6 pm. Branch offices have a break between 12:30 and 3:30 pm, with short hours on Fridays and days before Jewish holidays. In addition to stamps, you may get telephone tokens (*asimonim*) and use the philatelic service, if you wish to update your stamp collection with some of Israel's beautiful issues. Telegrams may be sent from the post office's *mivrakah* (*Mivrak* is a telegram).

Pharmacy

The Israeli Pharmacy, *Bet Mirkaḥat*, is different from the American drugstore in that it sells only medicines and toiletries. Hours are similar to those of other stores and shops. Learn to recognize the Hebrew signs: פתוח (*patu'aḥ*—open) and סגור (*sagur*—closed).

There is always one pharmacy open all night, on Sabbaths and holidays for emergencies. These 'on-duty' pharmacies are listed daily in all the local newspapers. In case of an emergency, ask for the *Magen David Adom*, the Israeli Red Shield of David (equivalent to a local Red Cross), by dialing 101.

Grocery

Small grocery stores (*Ḥanuyot makolet*) still abound in Israel, though modern supermarkets are becoming more numerous. Some of the small groceries are open longer. The advantage of the supermarket to the tourist is that it is set up in the American fashion, so that you can pick out whatever you need without having to ask for it. For the system of weights, get acquainted with the metric system practiced in Israel (see the conversion chart at the end of the book). Milk is sold in soft plastic half-liter and liter containers. Bread is baked daily, and you have quite a variety—from rye bread to *Ḥalah* (on Fridays and before Jewish holidays), to delicious rolls (*laḥmaniyot*). Bread, which is extremely cheap, is sold by the whole *kikar* ('loaf'—not to be confused with *Kikar Dizengoff*, Dizengoff Circle, in the hub of Tel Aviv), or half a loaf (*ḥatzi* kikar). Dairy products are excellent in Israel. So take advantage of the variety of *leben*, the American-style plain yogurt.

Souvenirs

Souvenir shops are situated near the large hotels and at city centers. 'Maskit' and 'WIZO' shops are known to have native crafts; however, they are not cheap. The Old City of Jerusalem abounds with small shops which are ideal for bargain hunters.

A note on greeting

An answer you may hear to *Boker tov* is *Boker or!*—'have a bright day.'

4 Getting to places

Listen to the following dialogue found in the introduction to Unit Four in the tape. You may consider the conversation addressed to you, try to understand it, and perhaps to participate in it.

Small talk . . .

Narrator	Shalóm. Zeh atáh!	שלום. זה אתה!
You	Ken. Zeh aňi. Shalóm.	כן. זה אני. שלום.
Narrator	Mah shlomćha?	מה שלומך?
You	Hakól beśeder.	הכול בסדר.
Narrator	Atáh medabér ivŕit!	אתה מדבר עברית!
You	Ktzat!	קצת!

Have you done the assignment from Unit Three?

You	Éifo taḥańat ha'otobúsim?	איפה תחנת האוטובוסים?
You	Patú'aḥ o saǵur?	פתוח או סגור?
Narrator	Hataḥańah petuḥ́ah o seguŕah?	התחנה פתוחה או סגורה?
You	Hataḥańah petuḥ́ah o seguŕah?	התחנה פתוחה או סגורה?

Key words and phrases

Eich	How
Ani magi'a	(Do) I get, arrive

Lakonsulyah	To the American
Ha'amerika' it	Consulate
Lech	Go
Yashar	Straight
Ad	To, till
Sof	End
Hareḥov	The street
Pneh	Turn
Yaminah	To the right
Ve'aḥar kach	And later, then
Smolah	To the left

Conversations

Asking directions to get to the Consulate

Visitor Sliḥ́ah, eich ańi maǵi'a lakonśulyah ha'ameriḱa'it?

סליחה, איך אני מגיע לקונסוליה האמריקאית?

or

Visitor Sliḥ́ah, éifo hakonśulyah ha'ameriḱa'it?

סליחה, איפה הקונסוליה האמריקאית?

Stranger Lech yash́ar ad sof hareḥov; pneh yaḿinah, ve'aḥ́ar kach yash́ar sḿolah.

לֵךְ ישר עד סוף הרחוב; פנה ימינה, ואחר כך ישר שמאלה.

Key words and phrases

Lataḥanah hamerkazit	To the central station
Pashut me'od	Very simple
Me'ah meter	100 meters
Vesham	And there
Tireh	You will see
Mah amarta	What did you (s.m.) say?
Le'at	Slowly
Ani tayar	I am a tourist

Ani lo mevin Ivrit — I don't understand Hebrew

How to go to the central station

Visitor	Sliḥah, eich ani maǵi'a lataḥańah hamerkaźit? סליחה, איך אני מגיע לתחנה המרכזית?
Stranger	Paśhut me'ód! Lech yasḣar me'áh ḿeter. Pneh sḿolah, vesḣam tiréh et hataḥańah hamerkaźit. פשוט מאוד! לך ישר מאה מטר. פנה שמאלה, ושם תראה את התחנה המרכזית.
Visitor	Mah amarta? Le'át, bevakaśhah! Ańi taẏar. Ańi lo mev́in Ivŕit. Atah medaber angĺit? מה אמרת? לאט, בבקשה! אני תַּיָּר. אני לא מֵבין עברית. אתה מדבר אַנגלית?

Key words and phrases

Lemuze'on yisra'el	To the Israel Museum
Kaḥ	Take
Otobus mispar tesha	Number nine bus
Mimul	Across
Misredei hamemshalah	The government offices
Hayom	Today
Yom shishi	Friday
Bareḥov hasheni	On the second street
Hakartis	The ticket
Kartisim levikoret!	Checking tickets!
Monit sherut	'Service' cab
Monit "special"	Taxi, cab
Letaḥanat harakevet	To the train station
Reḥov Hess	Hess Street
Shloshim ushmoneh	(Number) 38
Lisdeh hate'ufah	To the airport
Be'erech	Approximately
Matayim	Two hundred

How to get to the museum

Visitor	Eich ańi maǵi'a lemuze'ón yisra'él?
	איך אני מגיע למוזיאון ישראל?
Passerby	Kaḥ otóbus mispár tesha. Hamuze'ón mimúl misredéi hamemshaláh.
	קח אוטובוס מִספר תשע. המוזיאון מִמול מִשרדי הממשלה.
Passerby	Hayóm yom shishí; hamuze'ón saǵur aḥaŕei hatzohoŕayim.
	היום יום שישי; המוזיאון סגור אחרי הצהריים.

How to get to the bus

Visitor	Eich ańi maǵi'a le'ótobus mispár tesha?
	איך אני מגיע לאוטובוס מספר תשע?
Passerby	Hataḥańah bareḥóv hasheńi smólah.
	התחנה ברחוב השני שמאלה.
Visitor	Todáh rabáh!
	תודה רבה!

Going by bus . . .

Passenger	Aťah maģi'a lemuze'ón yisra'él?	אתה מגיע למוזיאון ישראל?
Driver	Ken.	כן.
Passenger	Ќamah oĺeh hakarťis?	כמה עולה הכרטיס?
Driver	Ḥamiśhah vaȟetzi shkaĺim.	חמישה וחצי שקלים.
Inspector	Kartiśim leviќoret!	כרטיסים לביקורת!

. . . and by 'monit sherut'

Passenger	Sheŕut!	שֵׁירוּת!
Passenger	Aťah maģi'a lataḥańah hamerkaźit?	אתה מגיע לתחנה המרכזית?
Driver	Ken.	כן.
Passenger	Ќamah zeh oĺeh?	כמה זה עולה?
Driver	Shmońah shkaĺim.	שמונה שקלים.

. . . or by taxi 'special'

Passenger	Ťaxi!	טקסי!
	or	
Passenger	Mońit!	מונית!
Passenger	Letaḥańat haraќevet!	לתחנת הרכבת!
Passenger	Lemuze'ón yisra'él, bevakaśhah.	למוזיאון ישראל,בבקשה.
Passenger	Reȟov Hess shlośhim ushmońeh.	רחוב הס שלושים ושמונֶה.

By cab . . . to the airport

Passenger	Ќamah zeh oĺeh lisďeh hate'uŕah?	כמה זה עולה לשדה התעופה?

Driver Maťayim shkaĺim be'érech.

מאתיים שקלים בערך.

Key words and phrases

Kivun eḥad	One way
Haloch vashov	Round trip (going and coming)
Olim (pl. m.)	Cost
Yotzet (f.)	Leaves
Harakevet haba'ah	The next train
Ratzif	Platform

Going by train

Passenger Shnei kartiśim le-Ḥeífa.
שני כרטיסים לחיפה.

Attendant Kivún eḥad, o halóch vashóv?
כיוון אחד, או הָלוך ושוב?

Passenger Halóch vashóv, bevakasháh.
הלוך ושוב, בבקשה.

Passenger Kámah zeh oléh?
כמה זה עולה?

or

Passenger Kámah olím hakartiśim?
כמה עולים הכרטיסים?

Asking when the train leaves

Passenger Matáy yotzét harakévet le-Ḥeífa?
מתי יוצאת הרכבת לחיפה?

Attendant Harakévet haba'áh yotzét besha'áh aḥat aḥaréi hatzohoráyim.
הרכבת הבאה יוצאת בשעה
אחת אחרי הצהריים.

. . . and from which platform

Passenger Me'éizeh retzíf yotzét harakévet le-Ḥeífa?
מאיזה רְציף יוצאת הרכבת
לחיפה?

Attendant Retzíf mispár shnáyim.
רציף מספר שניים.

Loudspeaker Harakévet le-Ḥeífa yotzét be'ód shtei dakót meretzíf shnáyim.
הרכבת לחיפה יוצאת בעוד שתי
דקות מֵרְציף שניים.

Key words and phrases

Liskor — To rent, hire
Betaḥ! — Of course! For sure! Surely!
Lechamah yamim? — For how many days?
Leshavu'a — For a week

Meḥir meyuḥad	A special price
Elef vahamishim	One thousand fifty
Bli hagbalat kilometrim	With unlimited mileage (kilometrage)
Lo kolel	Doesn't include
Mas erech musaf	Value added tax
uvitu'aḥ	and insurance
Mekabel	Accept
Kartis ashray	Credit card
Anaḥnu mekablim	We accept
Kol	All
Kartisei ha'ashray	Credit cards
Hamafteḥot	The keys
Nesi'ah ne'imah uvetuḥah	Have a pleasant and safe journey

Renting a car

Customer Efśhar lisḱor mechońit?
אפשר לשכור מכונית?

or

Customer Efśhar lisḱor óto?
אפשר לשכור אותו?

Agent B́etaḥ! Át́ah rot́zeh mechońit gedoĺah o mechońit ketańah?
בֶּטח! אתה רוצה מכונית גדולה
או מכונית קטנה?

Customer Mechońit ketańah.
מכונית קטנה.

Agent Lećhamah yaḿim?
לכמה ימים?

Customer Leshav́u'a. Ḱamah zeh oĺeh?
לשבוע. כמה זה עוֹלה?

Agent Yesh ĺanu meḥ́ir meyuḥ́ad: Elef vaḥamiśhim shkaĺim bli hagbaĺat kiloḿetrim. Lo koĺel mas érech muśaf, d́elek, uvit́u'aḥ.
יש לנו מחיר מיוחד: אלף
וחמישים שקלים בלי הגבלת
קילומטרים. לא כולל מס ערך מוסף,
דלק וביטוח.

Customer	Aťah mekabel karťis ashŕay?	אתה מקבל כרטיס אשראי?
Agent	Ken. Aňaḥnu mekablím et kol kartiśei ha'ashŕay.	כן. אנחנו מקבלים את כל כרטיסי האשראי.
Customer	Bevakaśhah.	בבקשה.
Customer	Efśhar lekabel et hamafteḥot?	אפשר לקבל את המפתחות?
Agent	Bevakaśhah. Nesi'áh ne'iḿah uvetuḥah!	בבקשה. נסיעה נעימה ובטוחה!

Key words and phrases

Letaḥanat hadelek hakerovah	To the nearest gas station
Sa	Go, travel
Bareḥov hashlishi	On the third street
Betzad yamin	On the right side
Al yad	Near
Haramzor	The traffic light
Tisa	You'll go; go; travel
Lakvish harashi	To the main road, highway
Baramzor harishon	At the first traffic light
Ḥatzi kilometer	Half a kilometer
Tireh	You'll see
Hashelet	The sign
Ḥeifa	Haifa

Asking for directions to the nearest gas station

Driver Eich ańi maǵi'a letaḥańat hadelek hakrovah?

איך אני מגיע לתחנת הדלק הקרובה?

Stranger Sa yaśhar bareḥov. Pneh smolah bareḥov hashliśhi. Hataḥańah betzad yamin, al yad haramźor.

סע ישר ברחוב. פְּנֵה שמאלה ברחוב השלישי. התחנה בצד ימין, על יד הרמזור.

or

Stranger Tiśa yaśhar bareḥov . . .

תִּסע ישר ברחוב . . .

. . . and how to get to the highway

Driver Eich ańi maǵi'a lakvish haraśhi le-Ḥeifa?

איך אני מגיע לכביש הראשי לחיפה?

Stranger Baramźor hariśhon pneh yamínah. Sa ḥat'zi kiloḿeter ad haramźor ḥasheńi.

Sham tiréh et haśhelet le-Ḥeifá.

ברמזור הראשון פנֵה ימינה. סע
חצי קילומטר עד הרמזור השני.
שם תראה את השלט לחיפה.

Key words and phrases

Shoter	Policeman
El	To (the)
Ha-Kotel Hama'aravi	The Western Wall
Bederech Ḥevron	On Hebron Road
Haḥomah	The wall (of the Old City)
Timtza	You'll find
Ḥanayah	Parking
Sha'ar Yafo	Jaffa Gate
Tikanes	You'll enter
La'Ir Ha'atikah	To the Old City
Derech	Through, by way of
Lech	Go, walk
Lefi	According (to)
Hashlatim	The signs

Asking how to drive near the 'Kotel'

Driver Shotér! Sliḥáh, bevakaśhah. Eich aní maǵi'a el ha-Kótel Hama'araví?

שוטר! סליחה, בבקשה. איך אני
מגיע אל הכותל המערבי?

Policeman Sa yaśhar beďerech Ḥevŕon ad haḥomáh. Timtza ḥanaýah al yad Śha'ar Ýafo. Tikańes la'Ír Ha-atikah ďerech Śha'ar Ýafo. Lech lefi hashlatím.

סע ישר בדרך חברון עד
החומה. תִמצא חניה על יד
שער יפו. תִכּנס לעיר העתיקה
דרך שער יפו. לך לפי
השלטים.

Driver Todah rabáh.

תודה רבה.

Assignment for next time

Think how to order a 'falafel' at the kiosk; order a half for your friend and a whole one for yourself. *Bete'avon!*— Have a hearty appetite! and *Lehitra'ot!*

Language summary

What you need to say

Asking directions to the American Consulate

Sliḥah, eich ani magi'a lakonsulyah ha'amerika'it?

Sliḥah, eifo hakon-sulyah ha'amerika'it?

. . . and to the central station

Sliḥah, eich ani magi'a lataḥanah hamerkazit?

Asking to repeat and slow down

Mah amarta? Le'at bevakashah!

Ani tayar. Ani lo mevin Ivrit.
Atah medaber anglit?

Asking how to get to the museum

Eich ani magi'a lemuze'on yisra'el?

Traveling by train

Shnei kartisim le-Ḥeifa

Haloch vashov, bevakashah
Kamah olim hakartisim?

Renting a car

Efshar liskor mechonit?
Efshar liskor oto?

Getting directions to the nearest gas station

Eich ani magi'a letaḥanat hadelek hakerovah?

Asking how to get to the highway

Eich ani magi'a lakvish harashi le-Ḥeifa?

. . . and how to drive near the 'Kotel'

Shoter! Sliḥah, bevakashah! Eich ani magi'a el ha-Kotel Hama'aravi?

What you need to listen for

How to get to the museum

Kaḥ otobus mispar tesha
Hamuze'on mimul misredei hamemshalah
Hayom yom shishi; hamuze'on sagur aḥarei hatzohorayim

Going by bus

Kartisim levikoret!

. . . and by train

Kivun eḥad, o haloch vashov?
Harakevet haba'ah yotzet besha'ah aḥat aḥarei hatzohorayim
Retzif mispar shnayim
Harakevet le-Ḥeifa yotzet be'od shtei dakot meretzif shnayim

Renting a car

Atah rotzeh mechonit gedolah o mechonit ketanah?
Lechamah yamim?

How to drive near the 'Kotel'

Sa yashar bederech Ḥevron ad haḥomah. Timtza ḥanayah al yad Sha'ar Yafo. Tikanes la'Ir Ha-atikah derech Sha'ar Yafo. Lech lefi hashlatim

Explanations

Some more imperatives

Lech yashar	*Go* straight
Pneh yaminah	*Turn* to the right
Kaḥ otobus mispar tesha	*Take* bus number nine
Sa yashar bareḥov	*Go* (*drive*) straight down the street

Adverbs

yashar *yaminah* *smolah*

The *ah* ending does not indicate feminine gender but direction: *to the left* and *to the right.*

Be'erech	Approximately
Betaḥ!	Surely, certainly!
Kan, po	Here
Derech	Through

Demonstrative

Et zeh	This
Kamah zeholeh	How much does this cost?

More questions

Eich ani magi'a lakonsulyah ha' amerika'it?	How do I get to the American Consulate?
Me'eizeh ratzif yotzet harakevet le-Ḥeifa?	From which platform does the train for Haifa leave?

Prepositions

In Hebrew, words like 'to', 'in', 'for', or 'at' often combine with the noun that follows:

lezug	*for* a couple
lelaylah	*for* a night

Sometimes the preposition and 'the' (*ha*) are combined:

balobi	*in the* lobby (*be'* + *ha* + *lobi*)
lakonsulyah	*to the* consulate (*le* + *ha* + *konsulyah*)

Other prepositions stand on their own:

im ḥalav	*with* milk

Numbers

1,000	élef	אלף
2,000	alṕayim	אלפיים
3,000	shĺoshet alaf́im	שלושת אלפים

4,000	arba'at alafim	ארבעת אלפים
5,000	ḥameshet alafim	חמשת אלפים
6,000	śheshet alafim	ששת אלפים
7,000	shiv'at alafim	שבעת אלפים
8,000	shmońat alafim	שמונת אלפים
9,000	tish'at alafim	תשעת אלפים
10,000	aśeret alafim	עשרת אלפים

Before the thousands the numbers appear in masculine and declined form; thus *shloshah* becomes *shloshet alafim*, although, one may use the first form in formal Hebrew, that is: *shloshah alafim, arba'ah alafim, ḥamishah alafim*, etc. But normally you should say: *shloshet alafim shkalim* (or *shekel*, in the singular), *arba'at alafim kilometrim, ḥameshet alafim liter*, and so on.

Dates

How do you tell historical dates? Years?

1492 *elef arba me'ot tishim Ushtayim.* Numbers are given in the feminine (except for tens, hundreds, and thousands, which have one form that does not change); the last number gets the 'and': *ve, va,* or *u.*

1776 *elef shva me'ot shivim veshesh* (or *vashesh*)

1948 *elef tesha me'ot arbai'im ushmonah*

Additional notes on use of numbers

buses	*otobus mispar tesha* (f.)
platform	*retzif shnayim* (m.)
address	*reḥov Hess shloshim ushmoneh* (f.)

And some high figures

100,000	*me'ah elef* (*elef* in singular!)
1,000,000	*milyon*;

Hebrew uses the term *milyard* for 'billion' (1,000 millions).

Days of the week		ימי השבוע
Sunday	*yom rishon*	יום ראשון
Monday	*yom sheńi*	יום שני
Tuesday	*yom shliśhi*	יום שלישי
Wednesday	*yom revi'í*	יום רביעי

Thursday	*yom ḥamiśhi*	יום חמישי
Friday	*yom shiśhi*	יום שישי
Saturday	*yom Shab́at*	יום שבת

Ordinal numbers — מספרים סידוריים

m.	*f.*		*נ׳*	*ז׳*
riśhon	rishońah	1st	ראשונה	ראשון
sheńi	shniýah	2nd	שנייה	שני
shliśhi	shliśhit	3rd	שלישית	שלישי
revi'í	revi'ít	4th	רביעית	רביעי
ḥamiśhi	ḥamiśhit	5th	חמישית	חמישי
shiśhi	shiśhit	6th	שישית	שישי
shvi'í	shvi'ít	7th	שביעית	שביעי
shmińi	shmińit	8th	שמינית	שמיני
teshi'í	teshi'ít	9th	תשיעית	תשיעי
asiŕi	asiŕit	10th	עשירית	עשירי

Telling the day of the week

Hayom yom rishon — היום יום ראשון
Hayom yom sheni, etc. — היום יום שני, וכו׳

Using ordinal numbers

a	*the*	*at the*
taḥanah	hataḥanah	bataḥanah
rishonah (f.)	harishonah	harishonah
taḥanah	hataḥanah	bataḥanah
shniyah (f.)	hashniyah	hashniyah
reḥov	hareḥov	bareḥov
shlishi (m.)	hashlishi	hashlishi
ramzor	haramzor	baramzor
revi'i (m.)	harevi'i	harevi'i

Ordinal numbers must agree with noun in gender (masculine or feminine), number (singular or plural) and article (definite or indefinite).

Other words related to time

shavu'a	week	שבוע
ḥodesh	month	חודש
shanah	year	שנה

Some expressions related to time

aḥar kach	later on	אחר כך
be'od	in a few . . .	בעוד
teichef	immediately	תיכף
miyad	at once	מיד
od me'at	in a little while	עוד מעט

Words related to directions and distances

yashar	straight	ישר
yamin	right	ימין
yaminah	to the right	ימינה
miyamin	on the right	מימין
smol	left	שמאל
smolah	to the left	שמאלה
mismol	on the left	משמאל
tzad	side	צד
al yad	near	על יד
lifnei	before	לפני
aḥarei	after	אחרי
karov	near	קרוב
raḥok	far	רחוק
po, kan	here	פה, כאן
sham	there	שם
mul, mimul	across	מול, ממול
derech	through	דרך
haloch vashov	round trip back and forth	הלוך ושוב
haloch veḥazor	round trip	הלוך וחזור

Worth knowing

The American Consulate

American Consulates are located in the three major cities in Israel. In Tel Aviv it is attached to the Embassy, at 71 Hayarkon St., not too far from the big hotels. In Jerusalem it is at 18 Agron St., and there are consulates in East Jerusalem and Haifa.

Central stations

In Jerusalem, the central bus station is located on Jaffa St., across from the Binyenei Ha'Umah Convention Center. The train station is at David Hamelech St., near the road to Bethlehem and Hebron.

In Tel Aviv, the central bus station occupies several city blocks near Hagalil St., a few blocks away from Petaḥ Tikvah Road. The central train station (to Haifa and Nahariyah) is at Arlozoroff St., near the diamond center; to Jerusalem and some southern towns, go to the Tel Aviv South Station.

In Haifa, the new bus station is close to the train station; they are both located in Bat Galim at the entrance to the city.

Buses

Public transportation within cities is serviced by Egged and Dan companies. Fares are low because service is subsidized by the government. It can be even less expensive if you buy a multi-trip ticket (25 or 23 for the price of 20) or a monthly ticket for 50 rides at a reduced rate. When you pay for a single ride, you get a ticket (which should be kept for inspection). Buses go from early in the morning (some start before 6 am) to late at night, depending on the locality. Buses stop running early Friday afternoon (particularly early in winter). There is no bus service on Sabbaths and Jewish holidays (except for some lines in Haifa, and in East Jerusalem). Service resumes at the end of the Sabbath or the holiday.

Monit sherut

Next to the central bus station is the 'monit sherut' service of cabs that follow certain bus routes and provide inter-city transportation. They cost a little more than a regular bus ride, but less than a 'taxi special,' called '*monit*' for its meter. While the 'monit' is a private cab, in a 'sherut' you have to share the ride with other passengers and go only on a certain route, stopping quite often. From the International Airport at Lod, there is an El Al bus service to (and from) the Tel Aviv central train station.

The only subway is in Haifa—the Carmelit, operating between the downtown area and Mount Carmel.

Trains

Trains between Haifa and Tel Aviv are very efficient and rather inexpensive. They operate from 6 am to 8 pm (some 13 trains a day, several of them express), getting to their destination in one hour. Fridays and days before Jewish holidays have special schedules. Round-trip tickets are more economical. Reserved seats in first class are available at extra cost. On Fridays and early Sundays, it is recommended that you reserve your seat to ensure a comfortable and pleasant ride.

Car rental

Car rental agencies are available at the airport and near the big hotels. If you pay in foreign currency or show your passport, some of the local taxes are waived. An American driver's license will do, but it is recommended that you get an international license, which is available through automobile clubs (AAA in the U.S.). Get acquainted with the rules of the road and with the major road signs and traffic regulations. Drive defensively. Members of AAA may get some service from the Israeli counterpart.

Rest rooms

You'll identify rest rooms by the double-zero sign (00) or by the male and female silhouettes. Cafés, hotels, and gas stations have modern facilities.

Holy places

When visiting holy places such as the Western Wall or Christian and Moslem shrines, dress modestly. At the Western Wall, men and women are required to go to their respective, separate sections for praying.

5 Eating out

Have you done the assignment from Unit Four?

You	Efśhar lekabel faĺafel eḥad?
	?אפשר לקבל פלפל אחד
You	Ve'ód ḥaťzi faĺafel, bevakaśhah.
	.ועוד חצי פלפל, בבקשה

Key words and phrases

Manah	Portion
Salat	Salad
Ḥamutzim	Condiments (pickled vegetables)
Teḥinah	Sesame seed sauce
Veharbeh	And a lot (of)
Ḥarif	Pungent, sharp, ''hot'', spicy (sauce)
Mitz	Juice
Kos	Glass
Gezer	Carrot
Bakbuk	Bottle
Shel	Of
Sodah	Soda water, seltzer
Gazoz	Flavored soda
Matok	Sweet
Ḥamutz	Sour

Conversations

Getting a falafel at a sidewalk kiosk

Customer	Ten li maṅah faĺafel, im saĺat,
	ḥamutzim, teḥinah, veharbeh ḥaŕif.
	,תן לי מנה פלפל, עם סלט
	.חמוצים, טחינה, והרבה חריף

Getting a cold drink

Customer	Mitz tapuźim, bevakaśhah. מיץ תפוזים, בבקשה.
	or
Customer	Kos mitz tapuźim, bevakaśhah. כוס מיץ תפוזים ,בבקשה.
Customer	Kos mitz tapuḥim, bevakaśhah. כוס מיץ תפוחים ,בבקשה.
Customer	Kos mitz agvaniýot, bevakaśhah. כוס מיץ עגבניות, בבקשה.
Customer	Mitz ģezer. מיץ גזר.
Customer	Ten li bakb́uk kaṫan shel Ćoca Ćola. תן לי בקבוק קטן של קוקה קולה.
Customer	Kos śodah, bevakaśhah. כוס סודה, בבקשה.

Customer Gaźoz, bevakaśhah.

גזוז, בבקשה.

Customer Efśhar lekabel kos gedolah shel gaźoz matok?

אפשר לקַבֵּל כוס גדולה של גזוז מתוק?

Customer Ten li kos ketańah shel gaźoz ḥamutz.

תן לי כוס קטנה של גזוז חמוץ.

Customer Shnei gaźoz. Eḥad matok ve'eḥad ḥamutz.

שני גזוז. אחד מתוק ואחד חמוץ.

Customer Ten li gaźoz eḥad; ḥamutz-matok.

תן לי גזוז אחד; חמוץ־מתוק.

Key words and phrases

Shulḥan	Table
Haḥalon	The window
Bapinah	In the corner
Tafrit	Menu
Atem Rotzim	You (pl. m.) want
Yesh lachem	You (pl. m.) have
Lemanah rishonah	For (the) first course

Ḥatzilim	Eggplant
Ḥumus	Paste of chick peas
Kaved katzutz	Chopped liver
Mah zeh?	What is it?
Mi yode'a?	Who knows?
Marak	Soup
Marak yerakot	Vegetable soup
Mah od?	What else?
Marak of ve'itriyot	Chicken soup and noodles
Umah od?	And what else?
Marak afunah	Pea soup

Having lunch at a Middle Eastern restaurant

Customer Shulḥán al yad haḥalón.

שולחן על יד החלון.

or

Customer Shulḥán bapinńah, bevakaśhah.

שולחן בפינה, בבקשה.

Customer Melťzar!

מלצר!

Customer Taffŕit, bevakaśhah.

תפריט, בבקשה.

or

Customer Efśhar lekabél taffŕit?

אפשר לקבל תפריט?

Ordering the first course

Waiter Mah atém rotźim lemańah rishońah?

מה אתם רוצים למנה ראשונה?

Customer Mah yesh laćhem lemańah rishońah?

מה יש לכם למנה ראשונה?

Waiter Lemańah rishońah: Ḥatziĺim, teḥinah, ḥumus, o kaved katzutz.

למנה ראשונה: חצילים, טחינה,
חומוס, או כבד קצוץ.

Customer Mah zeh 'ḥatziĺim'?

מה זה 'חצילים'?

Waiter Ḥatziĺim zeh . . . tov me'ód . . . zeh metzuýan . . .

חצילים זה . . . טוב מאוד . . . זה
מצויין . . .

Customer Mah zeh 'ḥatziĺim' be'angĺit?

מה זה 'חצילים' באנגלית?

Waiter Ańi lo yóde'a . . .
Mi yóde'a mah zeh 'ḥatziĺim' be'angĺit?

אני לא יודע . . .
מי יודע מה זה 'חצילים' באנגלית?

Owner 'Ḥatziĺim' zeh 'eggplant.'

'חצילים' זה 'eggplant'.

Customer Ten li ḥatziĺim uteḥinah lemańah rishońah.

תן לי חצילים וטחינה למנה ראשונה.

Waiter Mah bishv́il hagev́eret?

מה בשביל הגברת?

Customer Kav́ed kaťzutz bishv́il hagev́eret.

כבד קצוץ בשביל הגברת.

. . . and the second course

Waiter Mah lemańah shniýah?

מה למנה שנייה?

Customer Mah yesh laćhem lemańah shniýah?

מה יש לכם למנה שנייה?

Waiter Yesh ĺanu mařak . . .

יש לנו מרק . . .

Customer Éizeh mařak?

איזה מרק?

Waiter Meřak yerak̛ot . . .

מרק ירקות . . .

Customer Mah od?

מה עוד?

Waiter Meřak óf ve'itriýot . . .

מְרק עוף ואיטריות . . .

Customer Umah od?

ומה עוד?

Waiter Meřak afuńah . . .

מְרק אפונה . . .

Customer Meřak yerak̛ot.

מרק ירקות.

Waiter Vehagev́eret?

והגברת?

Woman	Ańi lo rot́zah maŕak!	אני לא רוצָה מרק!
Man	Ańi lo rot́zeh maŕak!	אני לא רוצֶה מרק!

Key words and phrases

Lemanah ikarit	For (the) main course
Basar	Meat
Dag	Fish
Baklava	Nut and honey cake
Manah aḥaronah	Dessert
Bete'avon!	Have a hearty appetite!
Ha'ochel	The food
Kasher	Kosher
Manah Kefulah	Double portion
Glidat shokolad	Chocolate ice cream
Begavi'a	In a cone
Vanilah	Vanilla
Tut sadeh	Strawberry
Mapit	Napkin
Metzuyenet (f.)	Excellent

Ordering the main course

Waiter Lemańah ikaŕit at́ah rot́zeh baśar o dag?

למנה עיקרית אתה רוצה בשר או דג?

Customer Ańi rot́zeh baśar.

אני רוצה בשר.

Waiter Yesh ĺanu steik, kab́ab, shishĺik . . .

יש לנו סטייק, קבב, שישליק . . .

Customer Kab́ab, bevakaśhah.

קבב, בבקשה.

Waiter Vehagev́eret?

והגברת?

Woman Ańi rot́zah dag.

אני רוצה דג.

. . . and dessert

Customer Ten li b́aklava vekaf́e turḱi lemańah aḥarońah.

תן לי בקלווה וקפה טורקי למנה אחרונה.

Waiter Bete'av́on!

בתיאבון!

Customer Ḥeshb́on, bevakaśhah.

חשבון, בבקשה.

Customer Ḱamah zeh oĺeh?

כמה זה עולה?

Inquiring whether it is 'kosher'

Customer Ha'óchel kaśher?

האוכל כשר?

Waiter Ken. Ha'óchel kaśher.

כן. האוכל כשר.

Getting ice cream

Customer Mańah kafuĺah shel ḿoka chip, bevakaśhah.

מנה כפולה של מוקה צ׳יפ, בבקשה.

Customer Glid́at shokol̍ad begav́i'a.

גלידת שוקולד בגביע.

Customer Glid́at vańil begav́i'a.

גלידת וניל בגביע.

Customer Glid́at tut sad́eh.

גלידת תות שדה.

Customer Efś har lekab́el maṕit?

אפשר לקבל מפית?

Vendor Bevakaś hah.

בבקשה.

Customer Haglid́ah metzuýenet!

הגלידה מצויינת!

Vendor B́etaḥ!

בטח!

Key words and phrases

Efes	Zero
Hakav tafus	The line (is) busy
Hakav panuy	The line (is) unoccupied
Etzlechem	With you, by you (pl. m.)
Elecha	To you (sing. m.)
Kaḥ	Take
Nimtza	Are, am
Bamalon	At the hotel
Haketovet	The address
Shelcha	Your
Hame'asfim	Name of street in Tel Aviv
Mispar	Number
Kachah-kachah	So-so
Mashehu	Something
Ke'ev rosh	Headache
Lakaḥti	I took
Yoter gadol	Bigger
Mah nishma	What's new? (What is heard?)
Yihyeh tov	It will be O.K. (good)

Speaking to a friend on the phone

Tourist (*dialing*) Ḥaḿesh . . . shal̍osh . . . éfes . . . éfes . . . shḿoneh . . . aḥ́at . . .

חמש . . . שלוש . . . אפס . . .
אפס. . . שמונה . . . אחת . . .

Tourist Hakáv tafús.

הקו תפוס.

Tourist Ah! Hakáv panúy!

(dialing)

הא! הקו פנוי!

Tourist Haló. Medabér Brown. Efshár levakér etzléchem ha'érev?

הלו. מדבר בראון. אפשר לבקר אצלכם הערב?

Friend Betaḥ!

בטח!

Tourist Eich aní magí'a elécha?

איך אני מגיע אליך?

Friend Kaḥ monít. Éifo atáh nimtzá?

קח מונית. איפה אתה נמצא?

Tourist Aní nimtzá bamalón. Mah haketóvet shelchá?

אני נמצא במלון. מה הכתובת שלך?

Friend Reḥóv Hame'asfím mispár arba'ím vetésha.

רחוב המאספים מִספר ארבעים ותשע.

Visiting relatives and friends

Tourist Érev tov.

ערב טוב.

Friend Érev tov.

ערב טוב.

Tourist Mah shlomchá?

מה שלומך?

Friend Káchah-káchah . . .

ככה־ככה . . .

Tourist Máshehu lo beséder?

משהו לא בסדר?

Friend Yesh li ke'év rosh . . .

יש לי כאב ראש . . .

Tourist Kaḥ aspirín!

קח אספירין!

Friend Lakáḥti shnei aspirínim . . .
Veyésh li ke'év rosh yotér gadól . . .

לקחתי שני אספירינים . . .
ויש לי כאב ראש יותר גדול . . .

Tourist	Mah nishḿa?	מה נשמע?
Friend	Yihýeh tov . . .	יהיה טוב . . .
Tourist	B́etaḥ yihýeh tov!	בטח יהיה טוב!

Language summary

What you need to say

Getting a falafel
Ten li manah falafel, im salat, ḥamutzim, teḥinah, veharbeh ḥarif

. . . and a cold drink
Mitz tapuzim, bevakashah
Kos mitz tapuḥim, bevakashah
Kos mitz agvaniyot, bevakashah
. . . Mitz gezer . . .
Ten li bakbuk katan shel Coca Cola
Kos sodah, bevakashah
Gazoz, bevakashah

Having lunch
Shulḥan al yad haḥalon.
Shulḥan bapinah, bevakashah
Meltzar!
Tafrit, bevakashah

Getting ice cream
Manah kefulah shel moka chip, bevakashah
Glidat shokolad begavi'a
Glidat vanil begavi'a
Glidat tut sadeh

What you need to listen for

Ordering the first course
Mah atem rotzim lemanah rishonah?
Mah bishvil hageveret?

Explanations

More questions . . .

Mah zeh 'ḥatzilim'? What *is* 'ḥatzilim'?
The demonstrative *zeh* (this, m.) is used as an auxiliary 'is' in spoken Hebrew.

Mi yode'a?   Who knows?
Mah od?   What else?

Different meals have different names

aruḥat boker	breakfast	ארוחת בוקר
aruḥat tzohorayim	lunch	ארוחת צהריים
aruḥat érev	supper, dinner	ארוחת ערב
aruḥat shabat	Sabbath meal	ארוחת שבת
aruḥat ḥag	holiday meal	ארוחת חג

Restaurants

misadáh mizraḥit	Middle Eastern restaurant	מסעדה מזרחית
misadáh ḥalavit	dairy restaurant	מסעדה חלבית
mitbaḥ tzarfati	French cuisine	מטבח צרפתי
óchel italḱi	Italian food	אוכל איטלקי
misadáh śinit	Chinese restaurant	מסעדה סינית

A very important number

éfes	zero	אפס

Worth knowing

Falafel has become the adopted Israeli national food. For a fast lunch or snack, you should try this Middle Eastern treat: falafel balls (made of ground, deep-fried chick peas) in round Arabic pita bread, to which you add a variety of vegetable salads, pickles of all sorts, *teḥinah* (a creamy sesame-seed sauce), and *ḥarif* (red, hot pepper sauce). Eating the falafel may be a 'messy' endeavor, so try it at a kiosk that provides tables, chairs, and napkins.

Tipping, while not required, is nevertheless practiced and is expected of tourists, especially in tourist places. Ten or fifteen percent is the norm. You don't have to tip cab drivers unless you get some extra service from them.

Reference section

Pronunciation guide

The Hebrew Alphabet

aleph	אלף	א
bet	בּית	בּ
vet	בית	ב
gimel	גימל	ג
dalet	דלת	ד
he	הא	ה
vav	וו	ו
zayin	זין	ז
ḥet	חית	ח
tet	טית	ט
yod	יוד	י
kaf	כּף	כּ
chaf	כף	ך כ
lamed	למד	ל
mem	מם	ם מ
nun	נון	ן נ
samech	סמך	ס
ayin	עין	ע
pei	פּא	פּ
fei	פא	ף פ
tzadi	צדי	ץ צ
kof	קוף	ק
reish	ריש	ר
shin	שׁין	שׁ
sin	שׂין	שׂ
tav	תו	ת

Consonants

א	a	
בּ	b	
ב	v	
ג	g	hard, as in 'go'
ד	d	
ה	h	
ו	v	

ז	z	
ח	ḥ	pronounced 'ch,' or more guttural (deep in the throat)—as in *ḥalva*
ט	t	
י	y i	
כּ	k	
כ ך	ch	as in 'loch' or 'Lech'
ל	l	
מ ם	m	
נ ן	n	
ס	s	
ע	a	some Israelis pronounce it as guttural
פּ	p	
פ ף	f	
צ ץ	tz	as in 'bits'
ק	k	
ר	r	hard
שׁ	sh	
שׂ	s	
ת	t	

Vowels and diphthongs

Vowels			Diphthongs		
a	as in	father	ei	as in	pay
e		set	ay		buy, night
o		off	uy		ruin
u		moon			
i		fee			

Notes

- Vowels tend to be long in spoken Hebrew. There is no distinction between short and long vowels in speech.
- The symbol ' separates two different vowels (but not diphthongs), as in *ve'asimon* (ve + asimon); each vowel is distinctly pronounced. The ' suggests a slight pause between syllables, as in the numbers shiv'ah, tihs'ah, shiv'im, tish'im.
- Each word in the Conversations sections (but not in the Language Summary sections) that has more than one syllable is accented (´) to indicate where the stress is placed: e.g., *shalóm* (say: *shaLOM*). In

spoken Hebrew you may hear a variety of stresses and accents. Even the word *shalóm*, when combined with *aleichem*, sometimes is accented on the first syllable: "*Shálom!*" (*SHAlom*).

- In words with *ah* and *eh* endings, the 'h' is silent: *todah* is pronounced *toda* (other examples: *rotzah—rotza; ugah—uga; tishteh—tishte*.
- The pronunciation of the letter 'ḥ' is similar to 'cha' and 'ech' (see above): ḥalav, tapuḥim, shaḥor, ḥeshbon, lehaḥalif. (Some Israelis pronounce the 'ḥ' from deep in the throat. This guttural sound is found in other Semitic languages, such as Arabic.)
- When 'e' appears in the first syllable of some words, it is pronounced with a very short sound, almost as if it weren't there: *geveret—gveret; petuhot—ptuhot*.
- Some Israelis pronounce 'e' as a diphthong ('ei'), as in *Mah hashem?—Mah hasheim?;* others pronounce 'ei' as 'e': *eich—ech; eizeh—ezeh*.
- The consonant ע is a guttural which is pronounced differently with different vowels: as 'a' in yode'a, tishah (say: tish-ah since accent is on last syllable), 'e' in mitzta'er, 'i' in nose'im, shiv'im (say: shiv-im), 'u' in ugah, 'o' in oleh, be'od. Although you don't have to use this guttural, it will help if you can recognize it.
- You may see the Hebrew letter 'ק' (kof) written as 'q' rather than 'k' in transliteration. Thus Ashkelon is Ashqelon. The sound, however, is the same.

Cross references

Language explanations (comments on grammar) are listed below according to subject matter and by unit number:

Accents	2
Adjectives	1, 2
Adverbs	4
Agreement and word order	1
And (conjunction)	2

Information provided in the Worth Knowing sections is listed below according to subject matter and unit number:

Conversion charts

Measurements and weights

Length

1 inch	2.54 cm.	1 cm.	0.39 in.
1 foot	0.30 meter	1 meter	3.28 ft.
1 yard	0.91 meter	1 meter	1.09 yard
1 mile	1.60 km.	1 km.	0.62 mile

Weight

1 oz.	28.34 gr.	1 gr.	0.035 oz.
1 lb.	0.45 kg.	1 kg.	2.2 lb.

Volume

1 pint	0.47 liter
1 quart	0.95 liter
1 gallon	3.8 liter

Temperature

Celsius	Fahrenheit
0	32
5	41
10	50
15	59
20	68
25	77
30	86
35	95
40	104

To get Fahrenheit from Celsius, multiply the Celsius reading by 9, divide by 5, and add 32 degrees.

Useful addresses

Israel Government
Tourist Office
Empire State Building
350 Fifth Ave.
New York, NY 10018

Consulate General of
Israel
800 Second Ave.
New York, NY 10017

Hebrew-English word list

Words are listed here as they appear in the book including prepositions, conjunctions and definite articles.

A

ad עד *until, to*
agorót (f.) אגורות *100 agorot in a shekel*
agvaniýot (f.) עגבניות *tomatoes*
aḥaréi hatzohoŕayim אחרי הצהריים *(in) the afternoon*
aḥat (f.) אחת *one*
al yad על יד *near*
anglít אנגלית *English*
ańi אני *I*
ańi lo meivín ivrít (m.) אני לא מבין עברית *I don't understand Hebrew*
ańi maǵi'a (m.) אני מגיע *I get (to a place), arrive*
ańi taýar (m.) אני תייר *I am a tourist*
arba'ím vetesha vaḥetzi ארבעים ותשע וחצי *49½*
aruḥat boker (f.) ארוחת בוקר *breakfast*
asimońim (m.) אסימונים *tokens*
at (f. sing.) את *you*
atah rotzeh (m. sing.) אתה רוצה *you want*
atem rotzim (m. pl.) אתם רוצים *you want*

B

ba'áretz בארץ *in the land (domestic)*
baboker בבוקר *in the morning*
ba'érev בערב *in the evening*
baḥamésh me'ót (f.) בחמש מאות *at (for) five hundred*
bakbuk (m.) בקבוק *bottle*
baklava בקלווה *nut and honey cake*
bamalon במלון *at the hotel*
bańanot (f.) בננות *bananas*
bapińah בפינה *in the corner*
bareḥov hasheńi (m.) ברחוב השני *on the second street*
bareḥov hashliśhi (m.) ברחוב השלישי *on the third street*
baśar (m.) בשר *meat*
bederech Ḥevrón בדרך חברון *on Hebron Road*
be'érech בערך *approximately*
beḿah uchal במה אוכל *with what (how) can I*
benzín tishím ve'eḥad בנזין תשעים ואחד *regular gas (91 octane)*

benzín tishím ve'árba'ah בנזין תשעים וארבעה *high-octane gas (94 octane)*
beśeder בסדר *O.K., fine*
hakol beséder הכל בסדר *everything is O.K.*
betaḥ! בתוח! *certainly!*
bete'avon! בתיאבון! *Have a hearty appetite!*
bishvíl בשביל *for*
bli hagbalat kilometrim בלי הגבלת קילומטרים *without limitation of miles (kilometers)*
boker tov בוקר טוב *good morning*
bulim (m.) בולים *stamps*
bulei בולי *stamps of*

D

dag (m.) דג *fish*
delek (m.) דלק *fuel, gas*
derech דרך *through, by way of*
do'ar avir דואר אויר *air mail*

E

éfes (m.) *zero*
efśhar אפשר *it is possible; (I) can; (I) may;* or (as question): *is it possible?*
efśhar lehaḥalif? אפשר להחליף? *can I change?*
efśhar leshalem? אפשר לשלם? *can I pay?*
eich איך *how*
éifo איפה *where*
ein li אין לי *I don't have*
éizeh (m.) איזה *which*
éizo (f.) איזו *which one*
el אל *to (the)*
élef vaḥamishím אלף וחמישים *1050*
érev tov (m.) ערב טוב *good evening*
esrim עשרים *20*
esrim liter עשרים ליטר *twenty liters*
esrím vaḥamiśhah shkalím (m.) עשרים וחמישה שקלים *25 shekels*
et zeh (m.) את זה *this*
etzleḉhem (m. pl.) אצלכם *with you, by you*
eliecha (m. sing.) אליך *to you*

G

gedolah (f.) גדולה *large*
geveret גברת *lady, Mrs.*
hageveret הגברת *the lady*
vehageveret והגברת *and the lady*
gezer (m.) גזר *carrot*
glidah (f.) גלידה *ice cream*
begavía בגביע *in a cone*
glidat shokolad גלידת שוקולד *chocolate ice cream*
vanilah וניל *vanilla*
tut sadeh תות שדה *strawberry*

H

ha'adon האדון *the gentleman*
ha'avír האויר *the air*
haḥalon (m.) החלון *the window*
haḥanuyot (f.) החנויות *the stores, shops*
haḥomah (f.) החומה *the wall* (of the Old City)
hakav tafus (m.) הקו תפוס *the line (is) busy*
hakav panuy (m.) הקו פנוי *the line (is) unoccupied*
hakartís (m.) הכרטיס *the ticket*
kartisím levikoret! כרטיסים לביקורת! *checking tickets!*

hakól beśeder gaḿur הכל בסדר גמור *everything is absolutely O.K.*
hakonśulyah ha'ameriḱa'it (f.) הקונסוליה האמריקאית *the American Consulate*
ha-Ḱotel Hama'araví (m.) הכותל המערבי *the Western Wall*
haketóvet (f.) הכתובת *the address*
hamafte'aḥ (m.) המפתח *the key*
hamafteḥ́ot (m.) המפתחות *the keys*
haḿayim המים *the water*
beḿayim במים *with water*
Hame'asfim *name of street in Tel Aviv*
hamḥa'ót nose'ím המחאות נוסעים *travelers' checks*
hamuśach (m.) המוסך *the garage*
hagaŕaj (m.) הגרז' *the garage*
ha'óchel (m.) האוכל *the food*
haradíator (m.) הרדיאטור *the radiator*
haramźor (m.) הרמזור *the traffic light*
baramźor harisḣon (m.) ברמזור הראשון *at the first traffic light*
harbéh הרבה *a lot*
hareḥ́ov (m.) הרחוב *the street*
hasha'áh shaĺosh השעה שלוש *it is three o'clock*
hasha'áh shḿoneh vaḥ́etzi השעה שמונה וחצי *the time is half past eight*
hasha'áh shḿoneh ushlośhim השעה שמונה ושלושים *the time is 8:30*
hasha'áh t́esha vaŕeva; hasha'áh ŕeva aḥaŕei t́esha השעה תשע ורבע; השעה רבע אחרי תשע *the time is a quarter past nine*
hasha'áh ŕeva let́esha השעה רבע לתשע *the time is a quarter to nine*
haśhelet (m.) השלט *the sign*
hashlat́im (m.) השלטים *the signs*
haśhemen (m.) השמן *the oil*
haýom היום *today* (*the day*)
hu הוא *he*

Ḥ

ḥafiśat aspiŕin חפיסת אספירין *a packet* (*pack*) *of aspirin*
ḥag saḿe'aḥ חג שׂמח *happy holiday*
ḥaḿutz (m. sing.) חמוץ *sour*
ḥamut́zim (m. pl.) חמוצים *pickled appetizers: pickled cucumbers, tomatoes, and peppers*
ḥanaýah (f.) חניה *parking*
ḥaŕif חריף *red, hot pepper sauce*
ḥat́zi kiloḿeter חצי קילו מטר *half a kilometer*
ḥatziĺim (m. pl.) חצילים *eggplant*
ḥ́eder eḥ́ad (m.) חדר אחד *one room*
ḥ́eder pańuy (m.) חדר פנוי *a vacant room*
ḥeshb́on (m.) חשבון *bill, check*
ḥ́etzi חֵצי *a half*
ḥ́umus (m.) חומוס *paste of chick peas*

I

im hamechońit עם המכונית *with the car*
im ha'óto עם האוטו *with the automobile*

im mitah kefulah (f.) עם מיטה כפולה *with a double bed*
ivrit עברית *Hebrew*

K

kabel odef (m. sing.) קבל עודף *accept change*
kachah-kachah ככה־ככה *so-so*
kadurei falafel כדורי פלָפֶל *falafel balls*
kafe shahor (m.) קפה שחור *black coffee*
  kafe turki קפה טורקי *Turkish coffee*
  nes kafe נס קפה *instant coffee*
  espresso אספרסו *espresso*
kah (m.) קח *take*
kamah zeh oleh? כמה זה עולה? *how much does this cost?*
  kamah zeh? כמה זה *how much is it?*
kan כאן *here*
kartis ashray (m.) כרטיס אשראי *credit card*
  kartisei ha'ashray כרטיסי האשראי *credit cards*
kashah (f.) קשה *hard*
kaved katzutz (m.) כבד קצוץ *chopped liver*
ke'év rosh (m.) כאב ראש *headache*
ken כן *yes*
kesef (m.) כסף *money*
ketanah (f.) קטנה *small*
kikar (m.) ככר *loaf*
kol כל *all*
kolel (m. sing.) כולל *including*
kos (f.) כוס *glass*
ktzat קצת *a little*

L

la'azor lecha (m. sing.) לעזור לך *to help you*
la'asot bishvilcha (m. sing.) לעשות בשבילך *to do for you*
lahtom לחתום *to sign*
  tahtom (m. sing.) תחתום *you'll sign (sign!)*
la'Ir Ha-atikah (f.) לעיר העתיקה *to the Old City*
lakahti לקחתי *I took*
lakvísh harashi (m.) לכביש הראשי *to the main road, highway*
latahanah hamerkazit (f.) לתחנה המרכזית *to the central station*
lavan (m.) לבן *white*
levanah (f.) לבנה *white*
laylah tov (m.) לילה טוב *good night*
le'amerika לאמריקה *to America*
lech (m. sing.) לֵך *go, walk*
lechamah? לכמה? *for how many?*
lechamah yamin? לכמה ימים? *for how many days?*
lefi לפי *according (to)*
lehamir להמיר *to convert, exchange*
lehem (m.) לחם *bread*
lehutz la'aretz לחוץ לארץ *to countries outside of Israel (abroad)*
lelaylah (m.) ללילה *for a night*
lelaylah ehad (m.) ללילה אחד *for one night*
lemanah ikarít (f.) למנה עיקרית *as a main course*
lemichtav (m.) למכתב *for a letter*
lemuze'ón yisra'él (m.) למוזיאון ישראל *to the Israel Museum*
leshavú'a (m.) לשבוע *for a week*
letahanat hadélek hakerováh (f.) לתחנת הדלק הקרובה *to the nearest gas station*

letaḥańat harakevet לתחנת הרכבת *to the train station*
harakevet haba'aḣ (f.) הרכבת הבאה *the next train*
leźug o leyaḥid? לזוג או ליחיד? *for a couple or for a single?*
ligluyáh (f.) לגלויה *for a postcard*
lisdéh hate'ufah (m.) לשדה התעופה *to the airport*
liskor לשכור *to rent, hire*
lo kolel (m. sing.) לא כולל *doesn't include*
lo nimtza kan (m. sing.) לא נמצא כאן *is not here*
lo yoda'at (f.) לא יודעת *don't know, doesn't know*
lo yode'a (m.) לא יודע *don't know, doesn't know*

M

mafte'aḥ (m.) מפתח *key*
hamafte'aḥ המפתח *the key*
maḣar מחר *tomorrow*
mah hasha'áh? מה השעה? *what is the time?*
mah haśhem? מה השם? *what is the name?*
mah nishḿa? מה נשמע? *what's new?* (*what is heard?*)
mah shimćha? (m. sing.) מה שִׁמְךָ? *what is your name?*
mah shmech? (f. sing.) מה שמךְ *what is your name?*
mah shlomćha? מה שלומְךָ? *how are you?* (to a male)
mah schlómech? מה שלומֵךְ? *how are you?* (to a female)
mah tishteh? (m. sing.) מה תשתה? *what would you like to drink?*
mah uchal? מה אוכל? *what can I?*
mah zeh? מה זה? *what is it?*
male מלא *fill* (*it up*)
malon מלון *hotel*
mańah (f.) מנה *a portion, a whole portion*
mańah kefulah מנה כפולה *double portion*
mańah aḥaronáh מנה אחרונה *dessert*
mapit (f.) מפית *napkin*
mar, adon מר, אדון *Mr.*
mařak (m.) מרק *soup*
meřak afuńah מְרק אפונה *pea soup*
meřak óf ve'itriýot מְרק עוף ואטריות *chicken soup and noodles*
meřak yerakot מְרק ירקות *vegetable soup*
mas érech muśaf (m.) מס ערך מוסף *value added tax*
máshehu lo beśeder? משהו לא בסדר? *is something wrong?*
matay מתי *when*
matayim מאתים *200*
matok (m.) מתוק *sweet*
me'áh מאה *100*
me'áh ḿeter מאה מטר *100 meters*
medaber (m.) מדבר *speak(s)*
medaberet (f.) מדברת *speak(s)*
ledaber לדבר *to speak*
meḣir meyuḥad (m.) מחיר מיוחד *a special price*
mekabel (m. sing.) מקבל *accepts*
ańaḥnu mekablím (m.) אנחנו מקבלים *we accept*
melafefońim (m.) מלפפונים *cucumbers*
meltźar מלצר *waiter*

meltzaŕit מלצרית *waitress*
metzuýan (m.) מצויין *excellent*
metzuýenet (f.) מצויינת *excellent*
miḿul ממול *across*
mirṕeset (f.) מרפסת *terrace, balcony*
misadah mizrahit (f.) מסעדה מזרחית *a Middle Eastern restaurant*
mish'hat shińayim (f.) משחת שִׁניים *toothpaste*
misredei hamemshalah (m.) משרדי הממשלה *government offices*
mitz (m.) מיץ *juice*
mitzta'ér (m.) מצטער *I am sorry*
mitzta'éret (f.) מצטערת *I am sorry*
mivŕeshet shińayim (f.) מברשת שניים *toothbrush*
mi yodé'a? (m.) מי יודע? *who knows?*
moníit (f.) מונית *taxi*
mońit sherút מונית שרות *service taxi*

N

nesi'áh ne'imah uvetuhah (f.) נסיעה נעימה ובטוחה (*have a*) *pleasant and safe journey*
nimtza (m.) נמצא *is*

O

o או *or*
otobus mispar tesha (m.) אוטובוס מספר תשע *number nine bus*

P

pańuy פנוי *unoccupied*
paśhut me'ód פשוט מאוד *very simple*
patu'ah (m. sing.) פתוח *open*
lo patu'ah לא פתוח *not open*
petuhot (f. pl.) פתוחות *open*
ṕitah (f.) פיתה *Middle Eastern pita bread*
pneh (m. sing.) פנה *turn*
po פה *here*

R

rakah (f.) רכּה *soft*
ŕega (m.) רגע *a moment;* (*wait*) *a minute*
rak ŕega רק רגע *one moment*
retzif (m.) רציף *platform*
rotźah (f.) רוצָה (*I*) *want*
rotźeh (m.) רוצֶה *want*

S

saǵur (m. sing.) סגור *closed*
sakit (f.) שׂקית (*soft plastic*) *container*
salat (m.) סלט *salad*
salat yerakot סלט ירקות *vegetable salad*
Śha'ar Ýafo שער יפו *Jaffa Gate*
shabat shalom שבת שלום *Good Sabbath; have a peaceful Sabbath*
shalom שלום *hello, hi, goodbye*
sham שָׁם *there*
shel של *of*
shelcha (m. sing.) שלךָ *your*
shem hageveret שֵׁם הגברת (*the*) *name of the lady*
sherutim שרותים *conveniences; private bath and toilet*
sheva (f.) שבע *seven*
shivím vahamiśhah (m.) שבעים וחמישה *75*
shloshah leilot (m.) שלושה לילות *three nights*

shloshím ushnáyim vaḥétzi (m.) שלושים ושנים וחצי 32½
shloshím ve'árba (f.) שלושים וארבע 34
shmonáh asár (m.) שמונה עשר 18
shotér שוטר *policeman*
shtéim esréh (f.) שתים עשרה 12
shulḥán (m.) שולחן *table*
sigaryót (f.) סיגריות *cigarettes*
  im filter עם פילטר *with a filter*
  bli filter בלי פילטר *without a filter*
smolah שמאלה *to the left*
sódah (f.) סודה *soda water, seltzer*
  gazóz (m.) גזוז *flavored soda*
sof סוף *end*

T

tafrít (m.) תפריט *menu*
tafús (m. sing.) תפוס *busy*
tapuzím (m.) תפוזים *oranges*
teḥínah (f.) תחינה *sesame seeds sauce*
tei im ḥaláv תה עם חלב *tea with milk*
  tei im limón תה עם לימון *tea with lemon*
  tei o kafé תה או קפה *tea or coffee*
ten (m. sing.) li תן לי *let me have*
tikanés (m. sing.) תכנס *you'll enter; enter*
timtzá (m. sing.) תמצא *you'll find*
tiréh (m. sing.) תראה *you'll see*
tisá (m. sing.) תסע *you'll go (travel); go*
titkashér (m. sing.) תתקשר *you should call*
tivdók (m. sing.) תבדוק *check; you will check*

todáh תודה *thank you*
  todáh rábah תודה רבה *many thanks*
tov (m. sing.) טוב *good*
  tov me'ód טוב מאוד *very good*
tut sadéh תות שדה *strawberry*

U

ugáh (f.) עוגה *cake*
  ugát duvdevaním עוגת דובדבנים *cherry cake*
  ugát geviňah עוגת גבינה *cheese cake*
  ugát tapuḥím עוגת תפוחים *apple cake*
umáh od? ומה עוד? *and what else?*
uvitú'aḥ (m.) וביטוח *and insurance*

V

ve'aḥár kach ואחר כך *and later, afterwards*
vechámah וכמה *and a few; and how many*
vegám וגם *and also*
vesham ושם *and there*

Y

yamínah ימינה *to the right*
yashár ישר *straight*
yesh lachém (m. pl.) יש לכם (*do*) *you have*
yesh lánu יש לנו *we have*
yesh lecha (m. sing.) יש לְךָ (*do*) *you have*
yesh li יש לי *I have*
yotzét (f.) יוצאת *leaves, departs*
yídish אידיש *Yiddish*
yihyéh tov יהיה טוב *it will be O.K.* (*good*)
yom shishí יום שישי *Friday*
yotér gadól (m. sing.) יותר גדול *bigger*

English-Hebrew word list

A

accept *mekab́el* (m. sing.)
  we accept *ańaḥnu mekabĺim* (m.)
accept change *kab́el ódef* (m. sing.)
according *lef́i*
across *miḿul*
the address *haket́ovet* (f.)
(in) the afternoon *aḥaŕei hat́zohoŕayim*
the air *ha'av́ir* (m.)
air mail *d́o'ar av́ir*
all *kol*
and a few *vecḣamah*
and also *veǵam*
and insurance *uvit́u'aḥ* (m.)
and later, afterwards *ve'áḥar kach*
and there *vesh́am*
and what else? *umah od?*
approximately *be'érech*
as the main course *lemańah ikaŕit* (f.)
at (for) five hundred *baḥaḿesh me'ót* (f.)
at the corner *bapińah* (f.)
at the hotel *bamaĺon* (m.)

B

bananas *bańanot* (f.)
be (is) *nimt́za* (m. sing.)
bigger *yot́er gad́ol* (m. sing.)
bill, check *ḥeshb́on* (m.)
bottle *bakb́uk* (m.)
bread *ĺeḥem* (m.)
breakfast *aruḥat b́oker* (f.)
busy *taf́us* (m. sing.)

C

cake *uǵah* (f.)
  cheese cake *uǵat gevínah*
  apple cake *uǵat tapuḥim*
  cherry cake *uǵat duvdevańim*
can I change? *efśhar lehaḥaĺif?*
can I pay? *efśhar leshaĺem?*
car *mechońit* (f.)
carrot *ǵezer* (m.)
check *tivd́ok* (m. sing.)
chopped liver *kav́ed kat́zutz* (m.)
cigarettes *siǵaryot* (f.)
  with a filter *im f́ilter*
  without a filter *bli f́ilter*
closed *saǵur* (m. sing.)
(soft plastic) container *saḱit* (f.)
coffe *kaf́e* (m.)
  black coffee *kaf́e shaḣ́or* (m.)
  Turkish coffee *kaf́e turḱi* (m.)
  instant coffee *nes kaf́e* (m.)
  espresso *esṕresso* (m.)
conveniences; private bath and toilet *sherut́im* (m. pl.)
to convert, exchange *lehaḿir*
credit card *kart́is ashŕay* (m.)
  credit cards *kartiśei ha'ashŕay*
cucumbers *melafefońim* (m.)

D

dessert *mańah aḥarońah* (f.)
(to) do for you *la'aśot bishvilćha* (m. sing.)
doesn't include *lo koĺel* (m. sing.)
don't know *lo yod́a'at* (f. sing.); *lo yod́e'a* (m. sing.)

E

eggplant *ḥatzílim* (m. pl.)
eighteen *shmońah asár* (m.)
end *sof*
English *anglít*
everything is absolutely O.K. *hakól beśeder gaḿur*
excellent *metzuýan* (m.); *metzuýenet* (f.)

F

faláfel *faláfel*
falafel balls *kaduŕei faláfel*
fifty-five *ḥamiśhim vaḥamiśhah* (m.)
fill it up! *malé!*
fish *dag* (m.)
five thirty *ḥaḿesh vaḥetzi* (f.)
the food *ha'óchel* (m.)
for *bishvíl*
for a couple or a single *leźug o leyaḥid*
for a letter *lemichtáv* (m.)
for a night *leláylah* (m.)
for a postcard *ligluýah* (f.)
for a week *leshavú'a* (m.)
for how many? *leĉhamāh?*
for how many days? *leĉhamah yaḿim?*
for one night *leláylah eḥad* (m.)
forty-nine and a half *arba'ím vetésha vaḥetzi*
Friday *yom shiśhi*
fuel, gas *délek* (m.)

G

the garage *hamuśach, hagaŕaj* (m.)
 the nearest garage *humuśach hakaŕov*
the gentleman *ha'adón*
give me; let me have *ten li* (m. sing.)
glass *kos* (f.)
go, walk *lech* (m. sing.)
good *tov* (m. sing.)
 very good *tov me'ód* (m.)
good evening *érev tov* (m.)
good morning *bóker tov* (m.)
good night *láylah tov* (m.)
good Sabbath; have a peaceful Sabbath *shabát shalóm*
the government offices *misredéi hamemshaláh* (m.)

H

a half *ḥetzi*
half a kilometer *ḥátzi kiloḿeter*
hard *kasháh* (f. sing.)
have a happy holiday *ḥag saḿe'ah* (m.)
have a hearty appetite! *bete'avón!*
have a pleasant and safe journey *nesi'áh ne'iḿah uvetuḥah* (f.)
he *hu*
headache *ke'év rosh*
Hebrew *ivŕit*
hello, hi, goodbye *shalóm*
(to) help you *la'aźor leĉha* (m. sing.)
here *po, kan*
hotel *malón*
how eich
how are you? *mah shlomĉha?* (m. sing.); *mah shlómech?* (f. sing.)
how much does this cost? *ḱamah zeh oléh?*
how much is it? *kámah zeh?*

I

I *ańi*
I am a tourist *ańi taýar* (m.)
I am sorry *mitzta'ér* (m.); *mitzta'éret* (f.)
I don't have *ein li*
I don't understand Hebrew *ańi lo meivín ivŕit* (m.)

get (to), arrive *ańi maǵi'a* (m.)
have *yesh li*
took *lakaḥti*
ice cream *glidah* (f.)
chocolate ice cream *glidat shokolad*
in a cone *begavia* (m.)
vanilla *vanilah*
including *kolel* (m. sing.)
in the evening *ba'érev*
in the land (domestic) *ba'áretz*
in the morning *baboker*
is not here *lo nimtza kan* (m.)
is something wrong? *mashehu lo beseder?*
it is possible; (I) can (I) may; or (as question): is it possible? *efshar*
it is three o'clock *hasha'áh shalosh*
the time is eight thirty *hasha'áh shmoneh ushloshim*
the time is half past eight *hasha'áh shmoneh vaḥetzi*
It will be O.K. (good) *yihyeh tov*

J
Jaffa Gate *Sha'ar Yafo*
juice *mitz* (m.)

K
key *mafte'aḥ* (m.)
the key *hamafte'aḥ*
the keys *hamafteḥot* (m.)

L
lady *geveret*
the lady *hageveret*
and the lady *vehageveret*
Mrs. *geveret*
large *gedolah* (f. sing.)
leaves, departs *yotzet* (f.)
let me have *ten li* (m.)
the line (is) busy *hakav tafus* (m.)
the line (is) unoccupied *hakav panuy* (m.)
a little *ktzat*
loaf *kikar* (f.)
a lot *harbeh*

M
many thanks *todah rabah*
meat *basar* (m.)
menu *tafrit* (m.)
Middle Eastern pita bread *pitah*
Middle Eastern restaurant *misadah mizraḥit* (f.)
a moment; (wait) a minute *rega* (m.)
money *kesef*
Mr. *mar, adon*

N
(the) name of the lady *shem hageveret*
napkin *mapit* (f.)
near *al yad*
number nine bus *otobus mispar tesha*
nut and honey cake *baklava*

O
of *shel*
the oil *hashemen* (m.)
O.K., fine *beseder*
everything is O.K. *hakol beseder*
on a diet *bediyetah*
on Hebron Road *bederech Ḥevron*
on the third street *bareḥov hashlishi* (m.)
one *áḥat* (f.)
one hundred *me'áh*
one hundred meters *me'áh meter*
one thousand fifty *élef vaḥamishim*

open *patu'aḥ* (m. sing.); *petuḥot* (f. pl.)
  not open *lo patu'aḥ*
or *o*
oranges *tapuźim* (m.)

P

a packet (pack) of aspirin *ḥafiśat* aspiŕin
parking *ḥanaýah* (f.)
paste of chick peas *ḥumus* (m.)
pickled appetizers: pickled cucumbers, tomatoes and peppers *ḥamutzim* (m. pl.)
platform *retzif* (m.)
policeman *shoter*
a portion, a whole portion *mańah* (f.)
  double portion *mańah kefulah*

R

the radiator *haradiator* (m.)
red, hot pepper sauce *ḥaŕif* (m.)
regular gas, 91 octane *benzín tishím ve'eḥad* (m.)
  high octane, 94 octane *benzín tishím ve'árba* (m.)
to rent, hire *liskor*

S

salad *salat* (m.)
  vegetable salad *salat yerakot*
on the second street bareḥov hashéni
sesame seed sauce *teḥinah* (f.)
seven *śheva* (f.)
seventy-five *shivím vaḥamiśhah* (m.)
the sign *haśhelet* (m.)
the signs *hashlatim*
to sign *laḥtom*
  you'll sign (sign!) *taḥtom* (m. sing.)
small *ketańah* (f. sing.)
soda water, seltzer *śodah* (f.)
  flavored water *gaźoz* (m.)
soft *rakah* (f. sing.)
sorry; I am sorry *mitzta'ér* (m.); *mitzta'eret* (f.)
so-so *kachah-kachah*
soup *maŕak* (m.)
  chicken soup and noodles *meŕak óf ve'itriýot*
  pea soup *meŕak afuńah*
  vegetable soup *meŕak yerakot*
sour *ḥamutz* (m. sing.)
speaks *medaber* (m.); *medaberet* (f.)
  to speak *ledaber*
a special price *meḥir meyuḥad* (m.)
stamps *bulim* (m.)
stamps of *bulei*
the stores, shops *haḥanuýot* (f.)
straight *yaśhar*
strawberry *tut sadeh* (m.)
the street *hareḥov (m.)*
sweet matok (m. sing.)

T

a table *shulḥan* (m.)
take *kaḥ* (m. sing.)
taxi *monít* (f.)
  service taxi *mońit sheŕut*
tea or coffee *tei o kafé*
tea with lemon *tei im limón*
tea with milk *tei im ḥalav*
terrace, balcony *mirpeset* (f.)
thank (you) *todah*
there *sham*
thirty-four *shlośhim ve'árba* (f.)
thirty-two and a half *shlośhim ushńayim*

vaḥetzi (m.)

this *et zeh* (direct object)

three nights *shloshah leilot* (m.)

through, by way of *derech*

the ticket *hakartis* (m.)
 checking tickets! *kartisim levikoret!*

the time is a quarter past nine *hasha'áh tesha vaṙeva; hasha'áh ṙeva aḥarei tesha*

the time is a quarter to nine *hasha'áh ṙeva letesha*

to (the) *el ha-; le*

to countries outside of Israel (abroad) *leḥutz la'áretz*

to the airport *lisdeh hate'ufah*

to the American Consulate *lakonsulyah ha'ameriḱa'it* (f.)

to the central station *lataḥanáh hamerkaźit* (f.)

to the Israel Museum *lemuze'ón yisra'él* (m.)

to the left *śmolah*

to the main road, highway *laḱvish harashi*

to the nearest gas station *lataḥanat hadelek hakrováh* (f.)

to the Old City *la'Ír Ha-Atikah* (f.)

to the right *yamínah*

to the train station *letaḥanat harakevet*
 the next train *harakevet haba'áh* (f.)

to America *le'amerika*

today (the day) *hayóm*

tokens *asimonim* (m.)

tomatoes *agvaniyot* (f.)

tomorrow *maḥar*

toothbrush *mivreshet shiñayim* (f.)

toothpaste *mish'ḥat shiñayim* (f.)

the traffic light *haramźor* (m.)
 at the first traffic light *baramźor harishon*

travelers' checks *hamḥa'ót nose'ím*

turn *pneh* (m. sing.)

twelve *shteim esreh* (f.)

twenty *esrim*

twenty-five shekels *esrim vaḥamiśhah shkalim* (m.)

twenty liters *esrim líter*

two hundred *matayim*

U

unoccupied *panuy* (m. sing.)

until, to *ad*

V

a vacant room *ḥeder panuy* (m.)

value added tax *mas érech musaf* (m.)

very simple *pashut me'ód*

W

waiter *meltźar*

waitress *meltzaṙit*

the wall (of the Old City) *haḥomah* (f.)

want *rotźah* (f. sing.)

the water *hamayim*
 with water *bemayim*

we have *yesh lánu*

the Western Wall *ha-Kotel Hama'araví* (m.)

what are *mah hen* (f.)

what can I *mah uḡal*

what is it? *mah zeh?* (m.)

what is the name? *mah hashem?*

what is the time? *mah hasha'áh?*

what is your name? *mah shimḡa?* (m. sing.); *mah shmech?* (f. sing.)

what would you like to drink? *mah tishteh?* (m. sing.)
what's new (what is heard)? *mah nishma?*
when *matay*
where *éifo*
which *éizeh* (m.)
which one *eizo* (f.)
white *lavan* (m. sing.); *levanah* (f. sing.)
who knows? *mi yode'a?* (m. sing.)
the window *hahalon* (m.)
with a double bed *im mitah kefulah* (f.)
with the car *im hamechonit*
with the automobile *im ha'óto*
with what can I *bemah uchal*
with you (by you) *etzlechem* (m. pl.)
to you *elecha* (m. sing.)
without limitation of miles (kilometers) *bli hagbalat kilometrim*

Y

yes *ken*
Yiddish *yidish*
you *at* (f. sing.)
(do) you have *yesh lecha* (m. sing.); *yesh lachem* (m. pl.)
you should call *titkasher* (m. sing.)
(Do) you want *atah rotzeh* (m. sing.); *atem rotzim* (m. pl.)
you'll enter *tikanes* (m. sing.)
you'll find *timtza* (m. sing.)
you'll go (travel) *tisa* (m. sing.)
you will see *tireh* (m. sing.)
your *shelcha* (m. sing.)

Z

zero *éfes*

ITINERARY

DATE	PLACE

EXPENSES

DATE	AMT.	U.S.$	FOR:

EXPENSES

DATE	AMT.	U.S.$	FOR:

PURCHASES

ITEM ________________

WHERE BOUGHT ________________

GIFT FOR ________________ COST __________ U.S.$ ____

ITEM ________________

WHERE BOUGHT ________________

GIFT FOR ________________ COST __________ U.S.$ ____

ITEM ________________

WHERE BOUGHT ________________

GIFT FOR ________________ COST __________ U.S.$ ____

ITEM ________________

WHERE BOUGHT ________________

GIFT FOR ________________ COST __________ U.S.$ ____

ITEM ________________

WHERE BOUGHT ________________

GIFT FOR ________________ COST __________ U.S.$ ____

ADDRESSES

NAME ____________________

ADDRESS ____________________

____________________ PHONE ____________________

NAME ____________________

ADDRESS ____________________

____________________ PHONE ____________________

NAME ____________________

ADDRESS ____________________

____________________ PHONE ____________________

NAME ____________________

ADDRESS ____________________

____________________ PHONE ____________________

NAME ____________________

ADDRESS ____________________

____________________ PHONE ____________________

ADDRESSES

NAME ______________________________

ADDRESS ______________________________

______________ PHONE ______________

NAME ______________________________

ADDRESS ______________________________

______________ PHONE ______________

NAME ______________________________

ADDRESS ______________________________

______________ PHONE ______________

NAME ______________________________

ADDRESS ______________________________

______________ PHONE ______________

NAME ______________________________

ADDRESS ______________________________

______________ PHONE ______________

TRAVEL DIARY

DATE________________

DATE________________

DATE________________

DATE________________

DATE________________

DATE________________

DATE________________

TRAVEL DIARY

DATE____________

DATE____________

DATE____________

DATE____________

DATE____________

DATE____________

DATE____________